LARE

SECRETS

Study Guide
Your Key to Exam Success

LARE Test Review for the
Landscape Architect Registration Exam

Published by
Mometrix Test Preparation
LARE Exam Secrets Test Prep Team

Written and edited by the LARE Exam Secrets Test Prep Staff

Printed in the United States of America

This paper meets the requirements of ANSI/NISO Z39.48-1992 (Permanence of Paper).

Mometrix offers volume discount pricing to institutions. For more information or a price quote, please contact our sales department at sales@mometrix.com or 888-248-1219.

ISBN 13: 978-1-5167-0549-8

Dear Future Exam Success Story:

Congratulations on your purchase of our study guide. Our goal in writing our study guide was to cover the content on the test, as well as provide insight into typical test taking mistakes and how to overcome them.

Standardized tests are a key component of being successful, which only increases the importance of doing well in the high-pressure high-stakes environment of test day. How well you do on this test will have a significant impact on your future- and we have the research and practical advice to help you execute on test day.

The product you're reading now is designed to exploit weaknesses in the test itself, and help you avoid the most common errors test takers frequently make.

How to use this study guide

We don't want to waste your time. Our study guide is fast-paced and fluff-free. We suggest going through it a number of times, as repetition is an important part of learning new information and concepts.

First, read through the study guide completely to get a feel for the content and organization. Read the general success strategies first, and then proceed to the content sections. Each tip has been carefully selected for its effectiveness.

Second, read through the study guide again, and take notes in the margins and highlight those sections where you may have a particular weakness.

Finally, bring the manual with you on test day and study it before the exam begins.

Your success is our success

We would be delighted to hear about your success. Send us an email and tell us your story. Thanks for your business and we wish you continued success-

Sincerely,

Mometrix Test Preparation Team

Need more help? Check out our flashcards at: http://MometrixFlashcards.com/LARE

TABLE OF CONTENTS

Top 20 Test Taking Tips

1. Carefully follow all the test registration procedures
2. Know the test directions, duration, topics, question types, how many questions
3. Setup a flexible study schedule at least 3-4 weeks before test day
4. Study during the time of day you are most alert, relaxed, and stress free
5. Maximize your learning style; visual learner use visual study aids, auditory learner use auditory study aids
6. Focus on your weakest knowledge base
7. Find a study partner to review with and help clarify questions
8. Practice, practice, practice
9. Get a good night's sleep; don't try to cram the night before the test
10. Eat a well balanced meal
11. Know the exact physical location of the testing site; drive the route to the site prior to test day
12. Bring a set of ear plugs; the testing center could be noisy
13. Wear comfortable, loose fitting, layered clothing to the testing center; prepare for it to be either cold or hot during the test
14. Bring at least 2 current forms of ID to the testing center
15. Arrive to the test early; be prepared to wait and be patient
16. Eliminate the obviously wrong answer choices, then guess the first remaining choice
17. Pace yourself; don't rush, but keep working and move on if you get stuck
18. Maintain a positive attitude even if the test is going poorly
19. Keep your first answer unless you are positive it is wrong
20. Check your work, don't make a careless mistake

Section 1: Project and Construction Management

This section deals with the role of the landscape artist as a communicator, team leader, and professional.

Landscape Architect

JOB DESCRIPTION

General duties include

- Provide professional services such as consultation, investigation, research
- Prepare general development and detailed site design plans
- Prepare studies
- Prepare specifications
- Provide responsible supervision related to the development of landscape areas
- Plan, preserve, enhance, and arrange land forms, natural systems, features, and plantings, including ground and water forms
- Project Manager
  - Qualified individual or firm authorized by the owner to be directly responsible for the day-to-day management and administration, and for coordinating time, equipment, money, tasks and people for all or specified portions of a specific project.
  - Review the work of others on his staff

Specific duties include

- Plan and design of vegetation, circulation, walks, and other landscape features to fulfill aesthetic and functional requirements
- Formulate graphic and written criteria to govern the planning and design of landscape construction development programs
- Prepare, review, and analyze master and site plan for landscape use and development
- Review environmental issues, population studies and public hearing schedules
- Analyze environmental and physical considerations related to land use
- Prepare drawings and construction documents
- Observe construction progress
- Evaluate construction documents prepared by persons working under the direction of the landscape architect
- Prepare feasibility studies, statements of probable construction costs, and reports and site selection for landscape development and preservation
- Integrate and determine the location of buildings, structures, and circulation and environmental systems
- Analyze and design
  - Site landscape grading and drainage
  - Systems for landscape erosion and sediment control
  - Pedestrian walkway systems
- Plan and place uninhabitable landscape structures, plants, landscape lighting, and hard surface areas

- Collaborate with other professionals in the design of roads, bridges, and structures regarding the functional, environmental, and aesthetic requirements of the areas in which they are to be placed
- Conduct field observation of landscape site construction, revegetation, and maintenance

Duties typically do not include
- Traffic, roadway, or pavement engineering
- Design of utilities
- Engineering of hydrologic management of storm water systems or floodplains
- Study of hydrologic management of storm water systems or floodplains
- Making of final plats
- Service or function within the practice of architecture, engineering, or public surveying

Construction Team

Allied Professionals
- Other state registered professions that are most similar to the practice of LA
- Traditionally includes licensed architects, professional engineers, land surveyors, professional planners, and interior design services

Building Inspector
- Assist builders, contractors, and owners by ensuring that construction projects meet building regulations and codes of practice
- Make on-site inspections during building work, checking that proper methods and materials are used which is reported to proper authority

Contractor
- An individual or company licensed to perform a defined scope of work on a construction project and agrees to furnish labor, materials, equipment and associated services to perform the work for a specified price

General Contractor
- Responsible for the execution, supervision and overall coordination of a project
- Hires specialty contractors for such tasks, e.g. electrical, plumbing
- Sees that the work is completed in a safe, technically competent and efficient manner

Specialty Contractor
- Licensed to perform a specialty task (e.g., electrical, side sewer, asbestos abatement)

Subcontractor
- Works for another general contractor

Trade Contractor
- Specializes in providing/installing specific elements of the overall construction requirements of a project

LICENSURE

Licensure refers to state licensing of individuals who have successfully met education, training, and formal examination requirements that indicate their competency to professionally practice landscape architecture. A license gives the legal right to practice in the certification area and a legal responsibility for the work projects.

State Landscape Architect Board
- Adopt necessary rules
- Set standards for licensure
- Adopt mandatory standards of professional conduct
- Investigate and discipline unauthorized, negligent or incompetent practice
- Act as an arbiter in a dispute between a LA and a member of the public

Council of Landscape Architecture Registration Boards (CLARB)
- National coordinating agency that was formed in 1961 that set guidelines for LA to guide state boards involved in licensing LA to practice.

REGULATIONS

If a state has a licensing law pertaining to landscape architecture, it can take one of two forms, a practice act or a title act.

Title Act
- No unqualified individual may call themselves a LA
- An individual may still perform the work of a landscape architect but not identify themselves as a landscape architect.

Practice Act
- Prohibits an unqualified individual from calling themselves a LA and from practicing the profession
- Strongest form of regulation to ensure the protection of the public health, safety, and welfare

Sunset law reviews
- "Sunset" involves the periodic review of state agencies that exercise the state's regulatory authority over occupations. Agencies are terminated by specified dates unless their life is extended by legislative action.

Reciprocal licensure
- Policy which acknowledges and accepts credentials awarded by another authority or jurisdictions
- Allows a landscape architect to serve a client in another state

RULES OF PROFESSIONAL CONDUCT

The following general and specific areas are typically addressed in codes of ethics adopted by state boards and which parallel the American Society of Landscape Architects (ASLA) Code of Professional Ethics.

Responsibility to the Public

- Make every reasonable effort to protect the safety, health, property, and welfare of the public
- Comply with all federal, state and local regulations
- Inform the employer or client of the possible consequences when the licensee's professional judgment is overruled under circumstances where the safety, health, property, or welfare of the public is endangered

Public Statements, Reports, and Testimony

May

- Express a professional opinion publicly on a landscape architectural subject only when that opinion is founded upon adequate knowledge of the material facts and a background of technical competence in the subject matter

May not

- Make statements or reports or give expert testimony on landscape architectural matters connected with public policy if the remarks are inspired or paid for by an interested party
- Precede any remarks made without the following
  - Identification
  - Disclosure of the identity of the party on whose behalf the remarks are being offered
  - Revealing the existence of any pecuniary interest in the matter
- Be untruthful, deceptive, or misleading

Competency for Assignments Undertaken or Approved

- May undertake to perform landscape architectural assignments only when qualified to do so by education or experience, or both

Conflicts of Interest

- Make every effort to avoid conflicts of interest with the employer or client
- Disclose promptly and fully all the circumstances to the employer or client whenever conflicts of interest appear unavoidable
- Inform promptly an employer or client of any business association, interests, or circumstances which may influence the judgment or the quality of services rendered to the employer or client
- Not accept compensation, financial or other, from more than one party for services on a project or for services pertaining to a project unless full disclosure is made by the licensee to all interested parties
- Not solicit or accept financial or other valuable consideration from a material supplier or equipment supplier for specifying the supplier's projects, except when the licensee is a previously announced employee or agent of the supplier
- Not solicit or accept gratuities, directly or indirectly, from any contractor, architect, engineer, or other party dealing with the licensee's employer or client in connection with work for which the licensee is responsible
  - Note: Gifts of only token value are acceptable

Improper Solicitation of Professional Employment
- Not compensate, give anything of value, or offer to compensate or give anything of value except for gifts of only token value and the usual commissions paid to licensed employment agencies
- Not falsify or permit misrepresentation of the licensee's qualifications or those of the licensee's associates when competing for professional employment

Knowledge of Improper Conduct by Others
- Not to conceal any information about the matter
- Not to refuse to divulge any information about the matter
- Not to make false or misleading statements about the matter

Seals and Rubber Stamps
- Not affix, or permit to be affixed name or seal to any drawing, specification or other document which was not prepared by licensee's or under personal supervision
- Not affix seal to any drawings, specification, or other document unless registrant has assumed the responsibility for the accuracy of the contract documents involved
- Affix any professional seal other than the licensee's own seal to a professional document

Causes for which licenses may be revoked

If the competence of a licensee to perform an assignment is questioned, the Board may require the licensee to submit to a formal or informal inquiry by or on behalf of the Board.
- Obtaining a licenses by fraud, deceit or misrepresentations
- Being guilty of fraud or deceit or of gross negligence or misconduct in the practice of landscape architecture
- Any professional misconduct, as defined by the board through bylaws, rules and regulations and standards of conduct and ethics (professional misconduct shall not be defined to include bidding on contracts for a price)
- Practicing or offering to practice landscape architecture on an expired license or while under suspension or revocation of a license unless said suspension or revocation be abated through probation
- Practicing landscape architecture under an assumed or fictitious name
- Being guilty of a felony
- Willfully misleading or defrauding any person employing him as a landscape architect by any artifice or false statement
- Affixing, or permitting to be affixed, the licensee's seal or name to any plans, specifications, drawings, or related documents which were not prepared by the licensee or under his or her responsible supervisory control
- Intellectual Property – property in the form of patents, trademarks, service marks, trade names, trade secrets, and copyrights.
- Having undisclosed financial or personal interest which compromises his obligation to his client
- Practicing in violation of the law or in violation of the proper rules and regulations of the committee
- Making any payment of money, except the regular fees, for the license
- Being adjudged mentally incapable by a court of competent jurisdiction

RIGHT TO HEARING

A licensed LA is entitled to a hearing if the board proposes to suspend, revoke, or refuse to renew a person's license. Administrative rules and regulations of state agencies are interpreted and applied by the Administrative Hearing Commission and the courts.

Administrative Hearing

A proceeding in which evidence is taken for the purpose of determining an issue of fact and reaching a decision on the basis of that evidence.

May take place outside the judicial process, before officials who have been granted judicial authority expressly for the purpose of conducting such hearings. (Landscape Architecture Board)

ROLE OF THE OWNER

- Provide evidence of the ability to pay bill
- Provide drawings with the description of the physical characteristics of the job
- Provide three copies of the drawings and project manual free of charge
- Make work area available at reasonable times
- Provide adequate space for materials and equipment
- Supply temporary utilities
- Provide vertical transportation to complete the job
- Authorize work stoppage if work is not in compliance with the contract
- Give a written notice to contractor to correct actions
- Carry out the work upon contractor failure to do so
- May perform work on own project with own work force
- May permit other contractors to do certain work on owner's project
- Provide obstacle free storage and work area and route
- Provide space and necessary equipment for the FF&E to be delivered, unloaded, prepped and stored
- Provide a schedule that is firm for the use of facilities to unload and transport the FF&E
- Inspect and verify that the FF&E order delivered is correct and free from damage
- Ensure security and safety of FF&E from the time of delivery to the final acceptance
- Refuse to accept order if found to be defective at a later date
- Comply with critical agreed upon schedule dates
- Accept responsibility for any loss to the contractor for failure to comply with agreed upon critical schedule dates
- Issues a change order
  - Process to change the work after the contract is signed
  - Written modification of the contract that affects the cost and schedule
  - Signed by owner, contractor and designer

ROLE OF THE CONTRACTOR

- Conduct pre-site inspection before delivery and installation
- Inform designer in writing if contractor notices nonconformity to stipulations in contract documents (otherwise will be responsible for cost to correct problems)

- Execute contract
- Develop, provide, and update schedule for owner's and designer's information
- Select non objectionable delivery route of FF&E
- Notify owner of special equipment needed to deliver and install FF&E
- Do all necessary work to install the FF&E which includes any cutting, fitting and patching
- Acquire written permission from the owner to alter the work of other contractors
- Coordinate schedule with other contractors
- Include an indemnification clause
- Provide job site safety
- Account for contractor's employees
- Account for subcontractors
- Avoid use/and/or damage to adjoining property
- Correct designer recommendations that do not comply with contract documents
- Not required to verify that the contract documents meet building codes, ordinances and any other local regulations
- Not responsible for damages caused by the owner or designer

Contract Law

Individual state statutes will often make references to contract law, lien law, and contractor licensing or registration law, indicating that each section of the law will help clarify how they work together and how they are affected by each other.

LIEN

A lien is a legal claim by one person on the property of another for security for payment of a debt.

Mechanic/Suppliers Lien
- A right given by statute to certain persons – typically suppliers, laborers, architects, etc. – who perform services improving real property.
- If they are unpaid, they may file a claim against the property and force the owner to pay even if the owner has already paid a prime contractor for their goods and services.

Preliminary lien notice
- Given to the property owner of a specific project by the subcontractors and any person or company furnishing services, equipment or materials to that project
- States if bills are not paid in full for the labor, services, equipment, or materials furnished or to be furnished, a mechanic's lien leading to the loss, through court foreclosure proceedings, of all or part of the property being so improved may be placed against the property even through the owner has paid the prime contractor in full

Claim of lien
- Usually must claim within 90 days after the last labor or material is supplied by a lien claimant

Payment of lien
- Not greater than the total amount of the contract price between the owner and the contractor, less the amount of payments made, if any, prior to the receipt of a copy of the lien by the owner

Lien release
- A written document from the contractor to the owner that releases the Lien, Mechanic's or Material following its satisfaction

Lien waiver
- Written document from a contractor, subcontractor, material supplier or other construction professional(s), having lien rights against an owner's property, relinquishes all or part of those rights

AVOIDING COMMUNICATION AND LEGAL PROBLEMS
- Use the most current standards available
- Include components that only apply to your project
- Use generally accepted wording when writing the standards
- Address only components for which you are responsible

- Separate the results from the methods to be used to accomplish the result
- Avoid describing project with subjective words or phrases such as best, first class, superior, and/or, and etc
- Address only one major topic per paragraph to facilitate reading and comprehension
- Be short

VALID CONTRACTS

There are six requirements necessary for a contract to be valid
- Usually consists of an offer and an acceptance of that offer
- Must have consideration which is something bargained for and given in exchange for a promise
- The parties must have the capacity, or legal ability to contract
- Both parties must be agreeable to the terms of the contract
- The subject matter of the contract must be legal
- Some contracts must be in proper form. Even though courts will enforce an oral contract, some categories of contracts must be in writing to be legal

LEGAL CONCEPTS

State statutes assign specific definitions to various legal terms.

Affidavit — A written statement in which the facts stated are sworn or affirmed to be true.

Arbitration — An arbitration agreement is a contractual provision whereby those bound to it give up their right to go to court and instead have any disputes underlying the contract resolved by an "arbitrator" or "arbitration panel."

Case law (Also known as **Common Law**) — A system of law that is derived from judges' decisions (which arise from the judicial branch of government), rather than statutes or constitutions (which are derived from the legislative branch of government).
- All Canada (except Quebec) and all of the United States (except Louisiana) follow common law.

Certify — Process of verifying that a record is complete

Commencement of improvements — First actual preparation or construction on the site, or the first delivery to the site of substantial materials.

Contractors — Person who contracts to do all or part of the work and retains control of means, method, and manner of accomplishing the work.

Deposition — A sworn statement of a witness or other party in a judicial proceeding.

Due Care — A theory of tort law to explain the standard of care or the legal duty one owes to others; what a reasonable person would do under like circumstances

Exoneration — This means a request to release the surety bond.

Improvements — Refers to all of or a part of the construction project. The statutes liberally define improvement as "any building, wharf, bridge, ditch, flume, reservoir, well, tunnel, fence, street, sidewalk, machinery and all other [applicable] structures or superstructures."

Interest holder — Those who share ownership of the property and/or improvements with the owner
- Includes: absentee owners, lessees, mortgagees (loan institutions or individual lenders)

License — A privilege or right granted to a person by a state to practice a profession.

Limit of Liability — The maximum amount for which an insurer is liable as set forth in the contract.

Lis Pendens — A recorded legal document giving constructive notice that an action affecting a particular property has been filed in either a state or a federal court.

Malfeasance — The doing of an act in an improper, wrongful, or unlawful manner.

Malpractice — A failure of a professional to act in accordance with the acceptable course of conduct, negligence of a member of a profession in a professional capacity.

Mediation — An informal means of trying to promote settlement of liability claim with a third-party mediator who meets with the parties and tries to get them to agree on a settlement.

Misfeasance — Performing a legal action in an improper way

Moonlighting — Used to describe the process of holding down a second job, usually during hours after the primary job is completed

Negligence — Failure to exercise that degree of care which an ordinary prudent person would exercise under the same or similar circumstances

Original contractors — Most state lien laws define original contractor as a contractor who has a contractual relationship with the owner. Commonly, the general contractor is the only one who has a direct contract with the owner.

Owners — Person who is, or claims to be, the owner of the land a portion of the land on which preparation or construction is performed.
- Person who entered into a contract for the purchase of an interest in the land or improvement being charged with a lien.
- Person who has a valid existing lease (lessee) on land or an improvement and who, on the basis of that lease, possesses an interest in the land or improvement.

Petition — A written request to the court for legal action, which begins a court case.

Reasonable Care — The amount of care expected of an ordinarily prudent person under the same or similar circumstances.

Reasonable care and skill — This generally means that any work done must be at least as good as the work of a competent person with average skills and experience in the type of work required.

Remand — The decision of an appellate court to send a case back to the trial court with instructions on how to correctly decide the case; often used with the term "reversed."

Standards of Practice — Guiding principles by which licensee's conduct their day-to-day responsibilities within their scope of practice.

Statue of repose — Set of laws used to define the maximum time period for filing claims against professionals.

Subcontractors — Not original contractors because they do not have a contract directly with the owner.

Summary judgment — Judgment entered when there is no genuine issue of material fact and party is entitled to prevail as a matter of law.

Statute of Limitations — The time limit within which a civil or criminal action may be brought after its cause arises.

Tort — A private wrong, independent of contract and committed against an individual, which gives rise to a legal liability and is adjudicated in a civil court.

Tort law — Tort law serves to protect a person's interest in his or her bodily security, tangible property, financial resources, or reputation. Interference with one of these interests is redressable by an action for compensation, usually in the form of unliquidated damages. The law of torts therefore aims to restore the injured person to the position he or she was in before the tort was committed (the expectation or rightful position principle).

Programming

CONCEPT

Architectural programming
Process of planning and designing a project

Design team
Consists of the following that must be licensed with the proper state licensing authorities where the facility is located.
- **Architect**
  - Primary designer of a building or project
  - Controls the overall design, specifications, finished materials (e.g., brick, paint, carpet, wall covering, etc.), and other architectural features of the building
  - Supervises the engineers
- **Engineers**
  - Responsible for the structural, mechanical, electrical, lighting and plumbing design of the building
  - Engineers must always conform to the design requirements of the architect.

Planning
- Initial stages of the design process
- Meeting among the architect(s) and engineer(s) and client
- Determines the following:
  - Purpose and objective of the proposed construction
  - Primary activities for which the project is being constructed
  - How the completed project relates to adjacent buildings (if any) and its surroundings

Preliminary Programming
- Produces a list of solutions, alternatives, feasibility studies and costs estimates.
- Results in preparation of schematic plans

Schematic Plans
- First plans of a facility
- Shows the interrelationship between spaces and activities
- Reviewed by all of the parties (architects, engineers, and the client)
- Make recommendations, as necessary
- Incorporated any changes into the final schematic plans
- Called revised schematic plans
  - Also known as preliminary plans
  - Provides a graphic view of the project, the refined details of how the project will look, and the relationship of all spaces.

Followed by the preparation of contract bid documents and working drawings.

Surveying

There are many kinds of surveys. The surveyor translates a legal description of a particular location into tangible positions on the ground.

TYPES OF SURVEYS

Title Insurance Coverage Survey
- Made for the purpose of supplying a title company and lender with survey and location data necessary for the issuing of title and/or mortgage insurance
- Determines property lines, location of improvements, identifying all easements, utilities and other conditions affecting the property

Archeological Survey
- Conducted to locate and/or investigate surface/subsurface archeological ruins
- Typically, magnetometers and side-scan sonars are used for offshore archeological investigations.

Boundary Survey
- Establishes the true property corners and property lines of a parcel of land
- Typically performed to obtain building permits, to resolve property disputes and to locate easement lines.

Cadastral Survey
- Original survey, resurvey, or retracement of public lands within the Public Land Survey System of the United States for restoration of property lines

Construction Survey
- Survey measurements made prior to or while construction is in progress to control elevation, horizontal position, dimensions, and configuration for buildings, fences, roads...
- Surveyor sets stakes for the proper location, elevation and relative placement of most types of infrastructure improvements
- Expressed and measured as distances to the east in meters (Eastings) and distances to the north in meters (Northings).

Control Survey
- Provides precise locations of horizontal and vertical positions of points for use in boundary determination, mapping for aerial photographs, construction staking, or other needs

Elevation or Floodplain Survey
- Determines the elevation of various sections of a building or land
- Typically used to aid in building plans and to determine if a property is in a flood zone

Geodetic Survey
- Takes into account the curvature of the earth and astronomic observations
- Uses a coordinate system for locating points on the earth
- Used on large scale planning projects

Global Positioning System (GPS)

A system of numerous Earth-orbiting satellites that can be used to determine the location (latitude, longitude and elevation) of a receiver or station on the Earth within about 2 m [(6') Fixed receivers on Earth can be used to determine the relative motions of fault blocks and lithospheric plates. Hand-held receivers can be used for producing accurate geologic maps, acquiring navigation data for 3D seismic surveys, and staking large-scale construction project (state highway)

Land Survey

- A survey of landed property establishing or re-establishing lengths and directions of boundary lines.
- Land boundaries are usually defined by ownership, commencing with the earliest owners through successive ownerships and partitions.

Laser Transmit

A transit in which a laser is mounted over the sighting telescope to project a clearly visible narrow beam onto a small target at the survey site.

Lot Line Adjustment (Boundary line adjustment)

Minor adjustment of a boundary line in order to transfer land between adjacent property owners

Lot Split Survey

- Needed for the division of an existing parcel of land into two or more parcels
- Includes a plat of the new parcels and a legal description to record the split

Lot Survey, (Site Plan Survey or Plot Plan Survey)

A combination of boundary and topographic surveys for preparation of a site plan to be used for designing improvements or developments and obtaining government building permits

Metes and bounds

- A time-honored land surveying method of describing land in terms of shape and boundary dimensions (Type of legal description of a lot)
- Typically used on small to medium landscape architecture projects

Plane Survey

- A survey in which the curvature of the earth is usually neglected
- The computations of relative positions of stations being made by plane geometry and plane trigonometry
- Used to develop cadastral maps
- Typically used for small to moderate size landscape architecture projects

Quantity Surveys

- Obtains measurements of quantities, usually in conjunction with a construction process, earthwork, etc.
- Oftentimes the Land Surveyor works closely with a Civil Engineer, Architect, or Landscape Architect.

Record or As-Built Survey
- Performed to physically locate structures and improvements on a parcel of land, generally for mortgage purposes
- Does not always include boundary monumentation

Registered Land Survey (aka R.L.S.)
A survey of "registered" (Torrens-title) land, usually done to shorten lengthy legal descriptions, or divide larger parcels of "Torrens-title" land into smaller tracts

Route Survey
Reconnaissance, preliminary survey and location survey for an alignment or linear type feature such as a road, railroad, canal, pipeline or utility line.

Subdivision Survey ("Subdivision Plat")
Subdivision of a tract of land into smaller parcels, showing monumentation and mathematical survey data on a map, conforming to local governing ordinances

Topographic Survey
- Locate natural and man-made features such as buildings, improvements, fences, elevations, land contours, trees, streams, etc.
- May be required by a government agency or used by engineers and/or architects for the design of improvements or developments on a site.

MAPS

The most convenient way to identify points on the curved surface of the Earth is with a system of reference lines called parallels of latitude and meridians of longitude. On most modern maps the meridians and parallels appear shown with minimum distortion. The UTM grid is shown on all quadrangle maps prepared by the U.S. Geological Survey (USGS).

Types
- 7.5-minute quadrangle maps (1:24,000 and 1:25,000 scale)
- 15-minute quadrangle maps (1:50,000, 1:62,500,
- Standard-edition 1:63,360 scales)

Grid Lines
- At intervals of 1,000 meters
- By blue ticks in the margins of the map or with full grid lines
- Show at 1,000-meter value for every tick or grid line
- Shows actual meter value for ticks nearest the southeast and northwest corners of the map

Tick Marks
- Blue numbered indexes located around the edge of a Topography Map.
- Accompanied with numbers like 3801, or 445, having 2 different sized characters representing the same number
- Spaced at a distance of 1 Kilometer (Klicks)

Hard corner

- Corner where both the latitude and longitude lines are marked as ending in 30" seconds
- Center of a 15 minute map of the same area
- Only one Hard Corner per 7.5 minute map

Declination Chart

- Located at the bottom of the Topography Map
- Shows the different angles between TRUE NORTH, MAGNETIC NORTH, and GRID NORTH

True North

- Directional line between any position on earth, to the True North Pole
- All lines of longitude are True North lines, and are also called `Meridian Lines.'
- Usually symbolized by an Arrow with a Star on a map

Magnetic North

- Direction to the Magnetic North Pole
- Actually the southern pole of the earth's central magnet, as is shown by the north seeking needle of a compass
- Usually symbolized by Half an Arrowhead

Grid North

- North that was established by the vertical grid lines during the map making process
- Usually symbolized by the letters GN or the letter Y

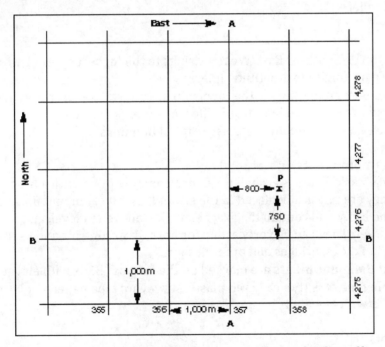

Example: The grid value of line A-A is 357,000 meters east. The grid value of line B-B is 4,276,000 meters north. Point P is 800 meters east and 750 meters north of the grid lines; therefore, the grid coordinates of point P are north 4,276,750 and east 357,800.

CONTOUR LINES

Contour lines are a method of depicting the 3-dimensional character of terrain on a 2-dimensional map. On multi-colored maps, they are usually brown. They join all heights of the same altitude together. There will be heavier contour lines every 4th or 5th contour line that are labeled with the height above sea level. The map legend will indicate the contour interval—the distance in feet (meters, etc.) between each contour line.

Contour Interval
- Difference between 1 contour line and the next
- This value is located at the bottom-center of map under the scale

Cliffs: Indicated by closely spaced contour lines
Depressions: Indicated by circular contour with lines radiating to the center
Gentle slopes: Less closely spaced contours
Ridges: Form a V-shape pointing down the hill
Steep slopes: Closely spaced
Summits: Form circles
Valleys: Form a V-shape pointing up the hill - these V's are always an indication of a drainage path which could also be a stream or river.

TRIGONOMETRIC SURVEY POINTS, or STATIONS

These are accurately surveyed places that are marked on a map that can help give an accurate idea of the land's actual relief.

Base Lines (BL)
- Tend to be North/South, or East/West bearings to the highest spots in an area but not necessarily true longitude or latitude lines.
- Results in an uneven meshing of the township lines at state lines, rivers and other borders when surveyors make base lines from different centers
- Example base lines: Mountain peaks, city capitol buildings

Bench Mark (BM) (monuments or stations)
A permanent "Bench Mark" (BM), is a small 6 X 6 inch concrete pillar with a brass USGS disk marker called a "tablet." They are physically placed in the ground, usually at mountain summits, but also in the flat areas around a city and contain the exact elevation above sea level, and the latitude and longitude of the marker. They can be vertical and/or horizontal controls and used to determine the exact placement of buildings, bridges and other designs.
- **Permanent BM monuments** are marked on the map as "BM x with elevation."
- **Recoverable markers** (typically red plastic surveyors tape nailed in place) are marked on the map as "x with elevation."

Horizontal Controls
- Usually appear only on maps along roads, near sea level, and in deserts where the contour lines are naturally widely spaced (very large flat areas of land).
- Always marked on the map with an "Triangle with elevation," or "BM Triangle with elevation"

Public Land Survey (USPLS)
- Area measurements which are public records used to record the value, extent, and ownership of land, as a basis for taxation.

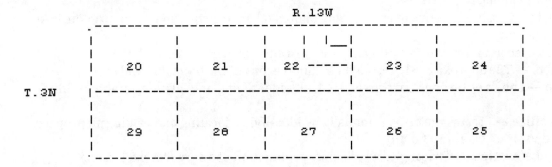

Quadrangle markings/Cadastral Coordinates/ Legal Descriptions
- Shown on Topo Map as very light red lines and numbers

Range
- Vertical row of townships, numbered East and West from a survey BL
- Numbered along both the top and bottom margins of the maps
- Numbered along the top and bottom margins of a map

Section of Land
- Each red outlined box, with its associated number.
- Equals 1 square mile (or 640 acres).

Note: Some federally owned lands, Indian Reservation property, Hawaii, Kentucky, Maine, Texas, Vermont, West Virginia, or District of Columbia, or the 13 original states do not show red boxes.

Township
- Squares in groups of 36 blocks which are repeated over and over again across the face of the map
- Each area of 6 x 6 `Sections of Land' is equal to 36 square miles. Townships are numbered along the left and right margins.
- Also super imposed over the map's regular contour line data.
- Numbered 1 through 36 beginning in the northeast corner of the township.
- Numbering of sections in a Township runs east to west across the first row of sections, then west to east across the second and alternately thereafter so that section 36 is in the southeast corner of the section.

Vertical Controls
- Show the height above average sea level
- Can be found anywhere, in walls, gate posts, sides of buildings, sides of trees

MAPS AND SURVEYING CONCEPTS

Acre — 208.7 feet = 43,560 square feet = 160 square rods

Aerial Photography — Photographs of a part of the earth's surface taken by a camera mounted in an aircraft for mapping purposes.

- Usually consists of a series of overlapping photos taken in strips which can form the basis for mapping
- Often used as an accurate way of determining a site's previous uses and uses

Aliquot Parts — The approximately rectangular subdivisions of the township and section.

Annotation — Labels or text on a map associated with identifying or explaining graphic entities shown

Assessor's office — Creates the tax roll annually by identifying, locating and valuing all property subject to ad valorem taxes in a County

Azimuth and elevation — Two angles which give the direction of a surveyor's telescope (theodolite).

- **Azimuth** is the rotation angle of the telescope around a vertical axis, measured (counterclockwise from above) from due north, a direction whose azimuth is 0°
- **Elevation** is the angle the telescope is lifted above the horizontal plane. [In 3-dimensional polar coordinates centered on the instrument, azimuth is f, elevation is 90°-q; the direction of straight up has elevation 90° but q = 0].

Backsighting — Process by which the surveyor checks for accuracy during the process of leveling once the equipment is set up and ready

- Examples: Manhole cover

Base Map — Refers to a map referenced to a coordinate system that depicts the fundamental map elements, such as Public Land Survey System section corners, streets, buildings, streams, etc., which are used for locational reference

Bearing — A unit of direction used in denoting the direction of a line bounding an area of land, usually measured in degrees (o), minutes ('), and seconds ("). It is a horizontal angle measured clockwise from north (either magnetic north or true north) to some point (either a point on a map or a point in the real world) bearing is measured clockwise.

Cadastral Data — The graphic and/or non-graphic data describing parcels which include property corners, boundaries, parcels of land, and related tabular attribute information.

Cartesian coordinates — A system of uniquely marking the position of a point on a plane [or in 3-dimensional space] -- by 2 numbers (its "Cartesian coordinates") giving its distances from 2 mutually perpendicular lines ("Cartesian axes"). The distances and the axes to which they are parallel are usually marked (x,y) in a plane and (x,y,z) in space; the "origin" is the point at which the axes intersect.

Chain/Chaining — Unit of length equal to 66' which is used especially in the U.S. public land surveys.

- Surveying tapes are often still called "chains" and measuring with a tape is often called "chaining." The chain is a convenient unit in cadastral surveys because 10 square chains equal 1 acre.
- Typically used to survey very hilly sites

Foresighting — Process the surveyor uses to determine a new point and elevation when looking through the instrument

Hub — Surveying marker that is magnetized for easy detection and zinc plated to resist corrosion. It has a large center point and looks like a standard survey marker.

Leveling — The surveying process of determining the difference in elevation between two or more points by measuring the vertical distance between two points.

- This is typically used to determine the topography of a site.

Link — Surveying measurement; 7.92"

Lot — Any portion, piece, division or parcel of land.

Marking Whiskers — An alternative marking choice for survey and construction sites, underground locating and many other uses. Also, they spring back up when run over by lawn mowers, graders and heavy equipment.

Meridian — A "line" on the earth's surface which follows the shortest distance from pole to pole.

Mile — 5,280 feet = 1760 yards = 80 chains

Parcel — A description of property formally set forth in a conveyance, together with the boundaries thereof, in order to easily identify it.

Parcel Number — The number assigned by a county to a parcel of property for identification purposes.

Plat (plot, map or chart) — A recorded map representing a piece of land subdivided into lots and blocks. Upon recording, and if complete, may transfer title to roads, streets, alleys, etc, May also create easements, etc.

Plat book (Recorded plat document) — Shows the location of all land in county by section/township/range numbers and in towns and cities by lot and block numbers. Sometimes showing name of owner, the road on which located, number of acres or dimensions of tract or lot, etc.

Plat map — A map of land ownership parcels for an area.

Plat Plan — Sometimes referred to as a plat map; usually a survey drawing of an individual parcel of land showing special characteristics and the location of any buildings thereon.

Point of beginning — The origination and destination of a Metes & Bounds legal description

Pole — 5.5 yards; 16.5'; one rod

Principle meridian — Longitudinal starting line from which range is measured to the East and West. In mapping the term has no definite meaning other than a map of a tract of country shown in rectangular format.

Quadrangle map (Quad) — A map with a roughly rectangular extent, defined by the four angles of its corners, which are often regularly spaced based on latitude and longitude.

- Often simply refers to a 7.5-minute map.
- Most show contours and elevations, highways, roads and other man-made structures, water features, woodland areas, bench marks, triangulation stations (some), geographic names, section lines, etc.

Quadrant — Any of four quarters into which something is divided by two real or imaginary lines that intersect each other at right angles.

- 90º of a circle; ¼ of a section (the NE ¼, NW ¼, SW ¼, and SE ¼ of a section are each quadrants of a section); one-quarter of a quarter section.

Quarter-Quarter-Section Corners — Corners placed on the section line midway between the quarter-section corner and the section corner (except on the last half-mile of section lines closing on the west boundaries of the township, or on other lines between fractional and irregular section). Few quarter-quarter corners were set in the original surveys of the U.S. public lands.

Quarter Section — A 160 acre block of land or ¼ of a section

Quarter Section Corner — Corners on a section line that were established halfway between the section corners

- Established and marked as part of the U.S. Public Land Survey

Quarter Section Lines — The lines that divide the sections into four parts

Quarter-section — 160 acres; usually identified as NE, SE, NW or SW.

Rod — A graduated staff used in determining the difference in elevation between two points. The two most common types of rods are the Philadelphia Rod, graduated in feet and hundredths of a foot, and a California Rod, graduated in feet, inches, and eighths of an inch.

Stadia measurements — Technique of distance measurement wherein the observer reads the intercept subtended on a graduated rod between two marks on the reticle of the telescope. It is based on the height observation of a 6' object.

Standard Section Diagram — A section contains 640 acres (258.99ha).

- One half of a section is 320 acres
- One quarter of a section is 160 ac (64.75 ha)
- One quarter of a quarter section is 40 ac (^{2}.19 ha).

Square mile — 640 acres

Terrain — The physical features of a tract of land.

Topography — The relief, elevation or shape of the earth in a given area

Traverse — A series of consecutive line segments whose lengths and directions are determined by field measurements.

- **Closed traverse** — either closes back upon its starting point, or begins and ends on stations of known positions.
  - Example: Property boundaries, Subdivision Plat
- **Open traverse** — does not close on either itself or a station of known position. (Should generally be avoided)
  - Example: Roads are typically open

Bidding

Bids or proposals are solicited from general contractors and/or specialty contractors.

PROCESS

Invitation to Bid
- Published in trade publications and newspapers by owners

Notice to Contractors
- Shown in the project's specifications
- Provides contractors with the bidding procedures

How a contract bid is prepared
- The contractor obtains a copy of the plans and specifications from the owner in order to prepare a formal estimate of the construction cost or bid (experienced construction personnel prepare the bids).
- The contractor reviews the contract plans and specifications to determine how to build the project and to consider all the limitations or conditions the owner requires for the project.
- The contractor solicits bids from subcontractors, estimates their direct material and labor costs, and evaluates the ultimate profit potential of the contract. The amount of the bid covers the estimated costs and a profit for the construction project.
- The owner evaluates all of the submitted bids and then awards the contract.
- The contract document and specs contain the project start and completion dates, the progress billing procedures, the insurance requirements, and other pertinent information.
- The preparation of a bid is the first step in the cost control system of a construction project. The agreed-upon bid price then becomes the budget by which the actual expenditures are measured and drawn against. The object of a cost control system is to provide the general contractor and/or owner with information regarding actual project costs versus the anticipated or budgeted costs. These cost comparisons become essential for internal control purposes.

Computing a bid

Cost estimating manuals
- Guides that contain a compilation of cost data for each phase of construction.
- For both union and non-union wage rates
- Used by subcontractors for specialty construction
- Examples: R. S. Means Building Construction Cost Data (highly detailed), Marshall Valuation Services

Estimators
- Use working drawings and specifications to estimate the project's construction costs
- Use subcontractor's and the material supplier's information

General contractor
- Has bank of information to estimate of labor and material costs.
- Gathers all the information from his estimators and subcontractors
- Adds in an amount for overhead and profit

Final cost estimate for competitive bidding
- Broken down and organized by the construction divisions shown in the specifications.
- Further detailed by trade and by item.

TYPES OF BIDS

Competitive Bid
- A process whereby an underwriter submits a sealed bid to the issuer.
- The issuer awards the contract to the underwriter with the best price and contract terms.

Lump sum
- Comprised of a one total price to complete all of the work
- Based on the Contractor's interpretation of the major items of work and the quantity or scope of each item

Unit price bids
- Based on predetermined major items of work, the items' quantities, and the Contractor's price per unit multiplied by the total quantity to create the total cost for each major item of work

Fixed-Price Contract
- Required contractor to perform the work described in the contract
- Price is not subject to any adjustment on the basis of the contractor's cost experience in performing the contract.

Cost-plus-fee contract
- Normally negotiated between the owner and the contractor
- In most cases, the owner pays actual costs of construction plus an additional amount based on a fixed percentage of the project's cost

PROCEDURES FOR MODIFICATION OF BID

Addenda (Addendum)
- Document that addresses changes or modifications made to the contract and issued prior to the bidding process
- Addresses questions, answers, errors and changes that evolve during the bidding process

Substitutions
- Process in which bidders request to use components other than the ones specified
- Approval results in an addendum sent to all bidders informing them of acceptable substitution

Alternate

- Request included in the bidding documents that asks the contractor to provide a price for some type of variation from the base bid which allows for flexibility in project cost.
- Usually allow space for add and deduct amounts in bid documents when necessary
  - Add-alternates - Request to add to the base bid
  - Deduct alternate - Request to reduce the base bid

NOTICE OF AWARD

- Written notice by the Owner to the apparent successful bidder stating that upon compliance by the bidder with the conditions presented in the notice the Owner will sign the Agreement.

NOTICE TO PROCEED

- Written notice from the Owner to the Contractor that establishes the date on which the Contractor shall begin performing its duties and obligations as outlined in the Contract Documents.

Budget

A budget is an estimate of probable expenses for a given project. It will include two kinds of expenditures: fixed and flexible.

Fixed or necessary expenses are those that occur regularly.

Flexible expenses are those that vary due to market factors.

DETERMINING INITIAL BUDGET

- Predetermined/fixed by client
- Predetermined/fixed by public funding/legislation
- Estimate based on client criteria

CRITERIA THAT AFFECT INITIAL BUDGET

- Size of project
- Quality of project
- Amount of money to be budgeted

COST FORMULAS

Fixed Price for the work

- Set price for the work

Time and Materials formula

- Specifies a price for different elements of the work such as, cost per hour of labor, overhead, profit, etc
- May state a "price not to exceed."

DETERMINING THE PROJECT COST (LARGE AND SMALL)

Preliminary Estimates

- Based on major systems or items, such as a water feature

Detailed Estimates

- Based on various components of design
  - Example: Patio furniture

Architect's Estimates

- Based on detailed items of various components as warranted by the available cost data
  - Examples: Piping and connections for water feature

Subcontractor Quotations

- Based on subcontractor quotation that involves a minimum amount of work for the general contractor

Quantity Takeoffs
- Process of developing most accurate type of budget
- Cooperative effort between the designer and general contractor
- Based on items of quantities that are measured (or taken off) from the engineer's plan that will result in a procedure similar to that adopted for a detailed estimate or an engineer's estimate by the design professional. May vary according to the desire of the general contractor and the availability of cost data

Construction Procedures
- Based on items such as labor, material and equipment needed to perform various tasks in the projects

Historical Cost Data (Cost books)
- Use of construction cost published in various forms by a number of organizations
- **Catalogs of vendors' data** on important features and specifications relating to their products for which cost quotations are either published or can be obtained
- **Periodicals** containing construction cost data and indices
- **Commercial cost reference manuals** for estimating guides
- **Digests** of actual project costs
  - Can provide detailed construction cost for labor and materials
  - Can provide parameter costs and subsystems costs
  - Can provide parameter costs for construction and furnishings
  - Provides an average cost for projects from different geographical regions
  - May not address specific project

Computer Aided Cost Estimation
- Numerous computer aided cost estimation software systems are now available
- Range in sophistication from simple spreadsheet calculation software to integrated systems involving design and price negotiation via the Internet.

Original budget
- Work backward from a set amount of money client has available
- Assign cost to various budget items

Cost per square foot
- Based on cost of similar project by designer or other contractors
- May or may not include various overheads, profit, taxes, contingencies

Local vendors in profession
- Familiar with local cost
- Familiar with doing similar projects

GUARANTEES

Refers to general financial forms that ensure that the monetary amount of the work will be met

Bonds

- Bonds include **bid, performance**, **payment (statutory)**, **maintenance** and other instruments of security.
- Provided by a surety company, the entity responsible for fulfilling the Contract in the event the original Contractor defaults for any reason
- Legal documents that guarantee to an Owner that the project
  - Will be completed
  - Is constructed properly
  - All labor, materials and equipment will be paid for in the event the contractor defaults on the original contract.

Bid Bond

- Submitted with the bid by the Contractor
- Security to the Owner that the successful bidder will enter into an agreement for the work and not withdraw or nullify its bid after submission
- Typical bid bonds are for 5% of the amount of the Contractor's proposal.
- In the event a Contractor desires to withdraw or nullify its bid, the Owner has the right to enforce its receipt of 5% of the bid price

Indemnification

- Part of an agreement that provides for one party to bear the monetary costs, either directly or by reimbursement, for losses incurred by a second party

Maintenance Bond

- Guarantees the Owner that any defects found after the work has been completed will be corrected by the original Contractor or other agent of the surety company

Performance Bond

- Guarantees the Owner that the project will be completed for the contract price in the event the original Contractor fails to perform the work

Payment (or Statutory) Bond

- Guarantees the Owner that all labor, equipment, and materials will be completely paid for in the event the original Contractor fails to perform the work

Prevailing wages

- On public projects with federal funding, the general conditions of a contract must include prevailing wages in the specification.
- Mean salary for one year of experience for the specific occupation and geographic location.

METHODS OF BILLING

Cost Plus or Cost Plus Fee Agreement
- Contractor is reimbursed for direct and indirect costs and, in addition, is paid a fee for its services.
- Fee is usually stated as a percentage of cost, but may be a fixed amount. The agreement may or may not include a guaranteed maximum price or a savings split.

Guaranteed maximum upset, billed hourly
- Sets a guaranteed maximum or ceiling price to the owner for the cost of construction

Percentage of construction cost
- Compensation is based upon a percentage of the construction cost
- Cost set by an estimate or bid

Percentage of prime consultant fee
- A method based on a portion of the project cost set using the prime consultant's fee amount in some percentage as the sub consultant's fee.
- Does not limit overall cost

Stipulated Sum Agreement
- A written agreement in which a specific amount is set forth as the total payment for completing the contract

Unit Price Contract
- Owner agrees to pay the contractor a specified amount of money for each unit of work successfully completed as set forth in the contract
- Includes all extra costs incidental to the item

Cash allowance/force account
- Establishes a purchase amount for miscellaneous items that cannot be specified during the bid stage

Reimbursement
- Payment made to someone for out-of-pocket expenses has incurred

PROGRESS PAYMENTS

All construction contracts extend over a period of time. The order of any business operation is to collect money as soon as work is complete. When a contractor completes a prescribed amount of work, the owner pays the contractor for the completed work.

Criteria for payment
- Must have **certification,** a written statement of the correctness and reliability of something; written permission to do something.
- Must be **notarized** application for payment
- Must be submitted (usually 10 days) before the date of each payment
- Must include value of work done to the date of application

- Must include the value of any unused purchased materials in acceptable storage
- Must be approved, certified and signed by the owner/designer before payment

Criteria for withholding payment
- Defective work
- Third party claims
- Evidence that the work
    - Is not verified by payment application information
    - Is not be completed according to contract documents
    - Cannot be completed with the remaining contract sum
    - Cannot be completed on time
    - Of others is not being paid
- Damage to the owner or another contractor

PAYMENT SCHEDULE

Pre-agreed upon schedule of payments to a contractor is usually based upon the amount of work completed
- May include a deposit prior to the start of work
- Often scheduled for the beginning of the month to allow the contractor to distribute to the subcontractors and suppliers by the 10th of the month.
- May also be a temporary 'holdout' at the end of the contract for any small items which have not been completed

ALLOWANCES

- A sum of money set aside in the construction contract for items which have not been selected and specified in the construction contract. Best kept to a minimum number and used for items whose choice will not impact earlier stages of the construction.
    - Example: Selection of tile

TYPICAL ITEMS NOT INCLUDED IN PROJECT BUDGET

- Design work
- Permits
- Specialty items such as utility hookups, lighting fixtures
- Loan fees and any special insurance
- Contingency amount

Construction Process

The construction process is a multi-step process that is similar in all locations when performed by a fee contractor, rather than an in-house labor force.

CONTRACT DOCUMENTS

The following information is detailed in contracts in order for potential builders to bid on the project:

Contract/Working Drawings/Plans

Architectural Plans
- Indicate the layout of the project, such as floor plans, elevations, and details of the construction and architectural finishes
- Typically numbered sequentially with the prefix "A" for "architectural"

Plan View
- An overhead view of the spaces on a specific floor
- Indicates the length, width and various heights of the structure and floor elevations
- May also contain details on a specific portion of work

Exterior Elevations
- Show the exterior and the exterior finishes
- Similar to photographs of the exterior

Architectural Schedules
- Indicates the flooring type, hardware, plumbing, and light fixtures in each space

Graphic Symbols
- Indicate various facility conditions
- Indicate the various types of material, sizes, and space finishes to be used

Site Plans
- Prepared by a civil engineer
- Includes the following:
  o Existing and proposed grades of the land
  o Specific location of the facility on the land
  o Proper drainage of a site
  o Design of land improvements, such as paving, curb and gutter design, retaining walls, and drainage culverts.

Structural Plans

- Prepared by structural engineers
- Shows the structural design of a building
- Incorporate foundation planning with considerations for rain, snow, wind, earthquakes, and other natural phenomena ("live" and "dead" loads)
  - **Live loads**
    - Consist of the people, furniture, and other items that are not part of the building, but are supported by the building.
  - **Dead load**
    - Weight of the building or structure itself

Mechanical Plans

- Prepared by a mechanical engineer
- Shows the design of the various mechanical systems in the building

Designed to incorporate the following:
- Proper air conditioning, heating, and ventilation equipment
- Adequate plumbing, to meet the needs for all of the building's designated activities
- Numbered with the prefixes "P" (plumbing) and "H" (heating, ventilating, and AC)

Electrical Plans

- Prepared by an electrical engineer
- Shows the electrical distribution system for power in a building
- Includes the distribution of electrical power from the utility company and the distribution to power-specific equipment
- Shows engineering design factors for the overall electrical "load" of a building
- Proper sizing and arrangement of transformers, panel boards, circuits, wires, conduits
- Power to the various machines
- Equipment and activities in the building

May also handle the following:
- Lighting design requirements of the building
- Specialty areas such as a central security monitoring system, a computerized control system, and fire and smoke management systems
- Number with the prefix "E" for "electrical"

Contract Specifications (specs)

- Instructs the contractor on how to build the project
- Consists of the following:
  - Contract documents
  - Technical specifications of the materials
  - Quality of the materials to be installed
  - Workmanship for installation of the materials
- Must be organized in a coherent manner due to the large amount of information that must be included
- Organized according to the CSI Master Format

BIDDING DOCUMENTS

Contract Form
- Dictates the form of the bidding conditions
- Divided into sections that include:
  - Agreement
  - Performance and Payment Bonds
  - Certificates

Contract Conditions
- Includes the General Conditions and Supplementary Conditions

Technical Specifications
- Generally prepared for each specific project in the CSI Master Format
- Includes hundreds, perhaps thousands of individual items that will be installed in the project

CONTRACT FORMAT

All parties involved in the construction project should be familiar with these documents and their role.

AIA Document A201, General Conditions of the Contract for Construction
Universally accepted in the construction industry
- Provides legal definitions of the elements in the construction process and the items that will be provided by the contractor
- Details how to prepare material submittals, shop drawings, and interim payment requests

Provides the legal basis and description of the following contract items:
- General Provisions
- Owner
- Contractor
- Administration of the Contract
- Subcontractors
- Construction by the Owner or by separate Contractors
- Changes in the Work
- Time
- Payments and Completion
- Protection of Persons and Property
- Insurance and Bonds
- Uncovering and Correction of Work
- Miscellaneous Provisions
- Termination and Suspension of the Contract

G702
- Provides the first basis for the construction cost control on a project
- Provides a breakdown and analysis of the construction costs
- Determines the basis for future release of funds for the progress (and ultimately the completion) of construction

Role of the Project Designer (Architect or Engineer)
- Review the G702 schedule of values prepared by the contractor to determine the accuracy of the cost allocations
- Provide adequate progress payment
- Pay for the completion of the project
- Accept or reject projects

Role of the contractor
- Breaks items of construction into as many parts as possible
- Completes the G702 by listing the total construction cost for each item of work completed to date
- Submits the G702 to request payment on a regular basis. Note: The more individual items of work that the contractor can identify and complete, the more items of work he/she will be entitled to bill and for which he/she will be timely paid.
  - Note: The amount previously paid for the work and the amount accomplished in this billing period are subtracted from the total amount to arrive at the amount of money remaining, minus a retainage (A portion of a contract payment that is withheld until contract completion to ensure full performance of the contract terms) for the completion of the work.

Role of Service examiner
- 3rd party who analyzes the G702
- May use cost manuals to estimate construction costs as part of the analysis of a study

CONTRACT

A contract is an agreement between two or more parties that is enforceable by law. As a legal document it specifies the what-when-where-how-how much and by whom in a construction project

Assignment
- Refers to the transfer of an obligation from one person or firm to another

Negation
- Refers to the canceling of a prior action

Contingency
- A provision that requires a certain act to be done or a certain event to occur before the contract becomes binding.

TYPICAL CONTENTS OF A CONTRACT
- Contractor's license (registration) number
- Names of all parties
- Addresses of all parties
- Phone, fax, email contacts and procedures
- Date of contract
- Property description
- Street address
- Subdivision

- Homeowners association
- Amount of contract
- Terms of financing
- Construction draw schedule
- Construction draw procedure
- Insurance requirements
- Start date and definition
- Substantial completion date and definition
- Plans, drawings, blueprints, sketches
- Specifications -as complete as possible
- Substitution policy
- Allowances - including labor and/or material
- Change order procedures and pricing
- Exclusions to the contract
- Authorized delay conditions
- Penalties or fines
- Access to the construction site
- Owner, lender, and third party inspection procedures
- Methods to solve disputes
- Arbitration clause
- Settlement terms
- Formal notification times and procedures
- Warranties and service policies
- Any documents required by state or local laws
- Signatures and dates of all parties on every page of every document with original copies for all signing parties
- Witness to all signatures and anything else about which two or more people can disagree, misunderstand, fail to do, install improperly, overlook, ignore, or that otherwise might create a problem between any or all of the aforementioned parties.

STATEMENT OF WORK QUALITY

Standard Practices of the Trade(s) (Most common)
- All relevant code
- Minimum standards of the trades or builder basic
- Standards of the trades
- Standards of the industry
- Manufacturer's specifications
- Craftsman like
- Custom construction
- Custom practices
- First class
- Top quality

According to Manufacturers Specifications
The written installation and/or maintenance instructions which are developed by the manufacturer of a product and which may have to be followed in order to maintain the product's warrantee

WRITTEN WARRANTY

In construction there are two general types of warrantees.

Manufacturer of a product
Example: Patio furniture
Labor
Example: A roofing contract may include a 30 year material warrantee and a 5 year labor warranty.

DISPUTES

A clause which outlines how any disputes will be resolved:

Binding arbitration
Parties agreeing to accept as final the arbitrator's decision

Nonbinding arbitration
Parties free to not accept the arbitrator's decision and to seek satisfaction through other means, including a lawsuit

Mediation
Parties agreeing to enter into good faith negotiations through a neutral mediator in order to attempt to resolve their differences

MODIFICATIONS TO CONTRACT

Any documented alteration in the specification, delivery, contract period, price, quantity, or other contract provisions of any existing contract, whether accomplished by unilateral action in accordance with a contract provision or by mutual action of the parties to the contract.

Change order or work change directive
Written document between the owner/designer and the contractor signed by the owner and the contractor which modifies (add, delete, or change) the plans and specifications and/or the price and the contract time of the construction Contract.

Contract amendment
A modification to a contract signed by the contractor as well as the contracting officer which provides for a change of contract provisions, including additional work outside the scope of the original contract.

FIELD ADMINISTRATION

Duties include attending to the following:

Inspection
- Periodically visit site in accordance with contract document

- Observe status of work to determine if the requirements of the contract documents are being met
- Make written report to client regarding progress and quality of work

Disputes
- Serves as impartial judge between the contractor and owner
- Renders decision regarding proper execution of work according to contract documents
- May request arbitration if either party is not satisfied with decision
- Must be in writing
- Must follow provisions stated in contract documents

Delays

Causes:
- Negligence of contractor (no additional time or money is allowed)
- Negligence of landscape architect or owner
- Change orders
- Labor disputes
- Fire

If not caused by contractor:
- May have extension of time
- May request additional fees to cover the delay

Stop-Work Order
A demand to stop an ongoing work activity due to a real or perceived dangerous operation or condition

MONITORING

Process of keeping track of the progress of the job to see if the planned aspects of time, fee, and quality are being accomplished

Units of Work Completed
For easily measured quantities the actual proportion of completed work.
Example: Work completed can be compared to the required amount to be completed.

Incremental Milestones
Particular activities can be sub-divided into a series of milestones, and can be used to indicate the percentage of work complete based on historical averages.

Opinion
Subjective judgments of the percentage complete can be prepared by inspectors, supervisors or project managers themselves.

Cost Ratio
- Cost incurred to date compared to what is budgeted
- Provides no independent information on the actual percentage complete

QUALITY CONTROL

Process of determining that design, cost and components of project meet the needs and requirements of the clients

Superintendent
A job title usually reserved for the administrative level person who supervises the work of an on-site contractor.

On-Site Inspector
Can witness the appropriateness/adequacy of construction methods at all times

Quality Circle
Composed of project principals who meet on a frequent basis to identify, discuss and solve productivity and quality problems.

Performance Specifications
Developed for many construction operations

Building Inspector/Official
A qualified government representative authorized to inspect construction for compliance with applicable building codes, regulations and ordinances.

INSTALLATION

Installation involves the planning, coordinating, and building the design

Role of contractor
- Make recommendation regarding rejection of any work that is damaged or does not meet contract documents
- Assist with the correct placement according to contract documents
- Answer questions that may arise

Role of the owner
- Provide delivery schedule and suitable space for the delivery, unloading, staging and storage of materials
- Inspect materials when delivered to identify and verify quantities as a basis for payment to vendors
- Provide security during storage and installation time against damage or loss
- Provide an unobstructed route to the final installment place
- Compensate contractor for any expenses occurred as a result of owner caused delays
- Inspect after final installation
- May reject damaged, defective, or nonconforming work found before final acceptance

PROJECT CLOSEOUT

The contractor begins process by inspecting work as follows.

- Determine the items to be completed or corrected
- Complete or correct list of items
- Determine if work is substantially completed, that stage in the progress of the work when is complete and in accordance with the contract documents except for completion of minor items that do not impair the owner from occupying and fully utilizing the work for its intended purpose
- Prepare a punch list, list of items to be completed or corrected by the contractor before Substantial Completion can be established.
- Complete or correct punch list
- Make a final inspection to verify that work is completed or corrected
- Submit application for final payment
- Assist owner with
  - Move-in
  - Operating manuals
  - Clean-up procedures
- Determine final completion that time when the work is fully completed and in accordance with the contract documents

POST-OCCUPANCY EVALUATION

Walk-Through

A final inspection of a home before "Closing" to look for and document problems that needs to be corrected.

- Review maintenance problems
- Look for defects covered under warrantees
- Evaluate design decisions
- Inspect durability of design decisions
- Determine owner satisfaction

INSURANCE

- Include clauses requiring the Contractor, and in some cases the Owner, to carry insurance to protect the public, property affected by or adjacent to the work, and financial interests of the parties involved in the project
- Usually located in the General Conditions and amended as necessary in the Supplementary Conditions

SUPPLEMENTAL DOCUMENTS

- Part of the Contract Documents where an Engineer or Owner can amend, modify, or supplement the Articles of the standardized GC
- May include the Invitation to Bid, the Instructions to Bidders, shop drawings and other written interpretations or clarifications such as minutes to pre-bid meetings
- Most commonly placed at the front of the bound project specifications and documents book

SCHEDULING

Completing a project in a timely manner is usually expected by the owner and provisions for timely completion for a project are often included in a contract.

Contract Time
- Refers to the period of time from the agreed upon starting date to the agreed upon substantial completion date
- Includes agreed upon adjustments
- May be extended by change order or circumstances beyond the contractors control

Date of Agreement
- Usually on the front page of the agreement
- If not on front page, it may be the date opposite the signatures when the agreement was actually signed
- When it was recorded
- The date the agreement was actually awarded to the contractor.

Date of Commencement of the Work
- The date established in a written notice to proceed from the owner to the contractor.

Daily Construction Report
- A written document and record that has two main purposes:
  - Furnish information to off-site persons who need and have a right to know important details of events as they occur daily and hourly
  - Furnish historical documentation that might later have a legal bearing in cases of disputes
- Should be as factual and impersonal as possible, free from the expression of personal opinions and feelings
- Should be numbered to correspond with the working days established on the progress schedule
- In the event of no-work days, a daily report should still be made, stating "no work today" (due to rain, strike, or other causes)

Date of Substantial Completion
Date certified by the architect when the work or a designated portion thereof is sufficiently complete, in accordance with the contract documents, so the owner may occupy the work or designated portion for the use for which it is intended.
- Can be stated as a specific calendar date
- Can be expressed as a number of calendar days from the date of commencement
- Terminates contractors schedule for the project which allows for bonuses or damages for late completion
- Has legal implications as in most cases it begins the statute of limitation of errors

Finish Date
Date that an activity or project is completed

Time is of the Essence

A provision in a construction contract by the owner that punctual completion within the time limits or periods in the contract is a vital part of the contract performance and that failure to perform on time is a breach and the injured party is entitled to damages in the amount of loss sustained.(e.g., "time is of the essence in the completion of the construction contract").

Timely Performance

Compliance with a time requirement

Timely Completion

Completing the work of the contract before the date required.

SCHEDULE CONTROLS

The following types of clauses are included in the contract to encourage the contractor to complete the project in a timely manner and according to plans.

Monetary

Liquidated damages

Specific sum (or a sum readily determinable) of money stipulated by the contracting parties as the amount to be recovered for each day of delay in delivery of the product

Bonus

Refers to a certain percentage of the payment that is awarded to the contractor for finishing the job ahead of schedule

Retainage (holdback)

Construction contract term for the funds that are earned by the contractor but not paid until some agreed upon date, such as the completion of the job

Shop drawings

Drawings, diagrams, schedules, and other data specifically prepared for the work, by the contractor or a subcontractor, to illustrate some portion of the work

Written interpretations

Clarifications are part of the Contract Documents

Transmittal

- Written document used to identify information being sent to a receiving party
- Includes cover sheet with the name, telephone/FAX number and address of the sending and receiving parties
- Includes a message or instructions

Assessment and Review

This section assesses the role of the landscape architect following the completion of the construction phase.

COMPLETION

The final phase of the construction process is known as the completion stage, and it readies the building for occupancy.

As Built Plans
- A set of plans prepared by the architect and contractor after a facility or project is completed
- Show exactly how the facility was constructed
- Includes all the changes to the original construction plan
- Represents the actual construction of the project
- Utilized when reviewing a cost segregation study

Notice of Partial Completion (Certificate/Notice of Partial Occupancy)
- Issued when inspection by local building officials determines that portion of the facility meets all building codes and is safe to be occupied
- Occurs when the owner desires to occupy a portion of the completed building
- Issued when inspection by local building officials determines that 95 % of the construction is complete

Notice of Completion/Certificate of Occupancy
- Issued when final inspection by local building officials determines that the building is 100% complete
- Followed when request by the contractor/owner after the building is 100% complete
- Recorded at the office of the local recorder
- Appraised for property tax purposes

Section 2: Inventory and Analysis

Land Use

Land use is the management of land to meet human needs. It includes rural, urban and industrial use. The landscape architect is required to have specific knowledge of local codes and standards and various regulatory requirements to carry out work. Knowledge of the following concepts is essential.

CONCEPTS

Abatement — The removal or elimination of a problem, nuisance, or other disturbance especially of public health or safety significance.
- Example: Allows for the removal of a site improvement not allowed by code.

Arterial Street — A street that generally has two or more moving lanes, traffic signals, may be designated a truck or bus routes, and is intended to serve traffic moving through an area.
- **Major Arterial**
  - Principal street within the network for the provision of both intercity and intra-city traffic movement.
- **Minor Arterial**
  - Secondary street within the network for the purpose of traffic movement between the neighborhoods and other areas within the city.

Area of state critical concern — Areas determined by local government and state and regional agencies which allow for the adoption of land development regulations, density requirements, and special permitting requirements by these entities.
EPA has delegated authority for implementing the Areas of Concern program to the states, including developing.
- Remedial Action Plans
- Coordinating with local public advisory councils
- Implementing cleanup activities

Building codes — Local regulations that control design, construction, and materials used in construction. These codes are based on safety and health standards.
Building (construction) permit — An authorization issued by a government agency allowing construction of a project according to approved plans and specifications.
Building Intensity Standards — The bulk and concentration of physical development of uses permitted in a district. Examples of measures of building intensity include the following:
- Lot coverage (LC)
- Floor Area
- Ratio (FAR)
- Open Space Ratio (OSR)
- Height, Landscape Volume Ratio(LVR)
- Building Volume Ratio (BVR)

Boulevard — Street lined with trees or constructed with a landscaped middle.

Buffer — Area of land which is set aside to provide transition between different land uses and to eliminate or reduce the adverse environmental impact, and incompatible land use impacts.
- Serves as a protective barrier

Capital Improvement — Any structure or component erected as a permanent improvement to real property that adds to its value and useful life.

Capital Improvement Program (CIP) — Long-range multi-year plan of capital improvement projects that are used in the development of annual operating and capital budgets, strategic plans, and long range financial plans.
- Provides the means for evaluating facility and infrastructure projects
- Provides expansion services such as street, sewer, and water projects that may affect a design plan
- Provides information on what services are to be upgraded, repaired, or constructed

Chicane — A series of narrowings or curb extensions, used at midblock locations only, that alternate from one side of the street to the other, forming S-shaped curves; a traffic calming technique.

Closures — A traffic calming technique including diagonal diverters, half closures, full closures and median barriers, the purpose of which is to reduce cut-through traffic by obstructing traffic movements in one or more directions.

Cluster Development — A pattern of development in which industrial and commercial facilities and homes are grouped together on parcels of land in order to leave parts of the land undeveloped Zoning ordinances permit cluster development by allowing smaller lot sizes when part of the land is left as open space. A component of PUD.

Collector Street — Streets that connect residential and local streets and neighborhood connector streets through or adjacent to more than one neighborhood and have continuity between arterial streets.
- Convey traffic out of the neighborhoods to the arterial streets

Comprehensive/Master plan — It is an official statement of a governing body which sets forth major policies concerning the desired future land use and physical development of an area. It describes the long-term direction and vision for growth and development. Topic areas typically include land use, economic development, community character, natural resources, parks and recreation, transportation, housing, and historic preservation. This long range plan outlines trends in the area and how to address future growth in areas such as transportation, environment, and recreation.

Covenant — A written agreement between two or more parties in which a party or parties pledge to perform or not perform specified acts with regard to property; usually found in such real estate documents as deeds, mortgages, leases and contracts for deed.
- **Restrictive Covenant**
  - An agreement included in a deed to real property that the buyer (grantee) will be limited as to the future use of the property.
    - Example: Fence building

Conveyance — A written instrument used to transfer (convey) title to property, such as a deed.

Cul-de-sac — Dead-end street with only one inlet/outlet and a turnaround area at its closed end which limits through-traffic in residential areas.

Deed — Document that transfers ownership of real estate
Contains the names of both the old and new owners, and a legal description of the property and signed by the person transferring the property (seller).

- **Deed of Trust**
    - o Legal document that conveys title to real property to a 3rd party
    - o The 3rd party holds title until the owner of the property has repaid the debt in full.
    - o In some states, a "deed of trust" is used instead of a mortgage.
- **Quit Claim Deed**
    - o Transfers to the grantee any and all of the legal rights the grantor has in the parcel of real property.
    - o Used to clear "clouds on the title"
        - ▪ Example: Misspelled name on earlier transfer of the property.

Demography — Statistical study of the characteristics of human populations, such as size, growth, density, distribution, and vital statistics as well as how populations change over time due to births, deaths, migration and ageing. This is used by landscape architects to analyze neighborhood characteristics, make neighborhood comparisons, and determine median income in order to determine housing needs during the initial stages of planning a project.

Density — The average number of people, families, or housing units on one unit of land Density is also expressed as dwelling units per acre.

Environmental Impact Report (EIR) — Public document used by a governmental agency to analyze the significant environmental effects of a proposed project, to identify alternatives and to disclose possible ways to reduce or avoid possible environmental damage.

Easement — A legal right or permission, giving a person or entity limited use of another's property. If the easement benefits the holder personally and is not associated with any land he owns, it is an easement in gross (e.g., a public utility's right to run power lines through another's property).
If the easement is held incident to ownership of some land, it is an easement appurtenant (e.g., the right to run a ditch through a neighbor's yard to drain your land).

- **Temporary Easement**
    - o A grant by a property owner to the public or other person or entity over specific tract of land for a specific use or purpose for a specific time frame.
- **Permanent Easement**
    - o A grant by a property owner to the public, over specific tract of land for a specific use or purpose of indefinite duration.
- **Scenic Easement**
    - o A legal means of protecting beautiful views and associated aesthetic quality along a site by restricting change in existing features without government approval.

Environmental regulations — Federal, state and local requirements for managing the nation's environmental health. The landscape architect would be primarily concerned with temporary and permanent measures for sediment and erosion control and wetland or stream protection.

Frontage — The boundary of a property which abuts an existing or dedicated public right-of-way, water body or similar barrier

Greenbelt/ Greenway — A corridor composed of natural vegetation with specific measures designed to mitigate fire, flood and erosion hazard, land use planning, and development

- Example: An irrigated landscaped buffer zone between development and wild lands such as golf courses, park, etc.

Intensity — A comparison of the development proposal against environmental constraints or other conditions which determine the carrying capacity of a specific land area to accommodate development without adverse impacts.

Land classification — Current law requires that Sixteenth Section Lands be classified into one of nine land classifications. The classifications are: Forest, Agricultural, Industrial, Commercial, Residential, Farm Residential, Recreational, Catfish Farming, and Other. Land classification is determined according to the highest and best land use that will produce the maximum income from leasing.

Land-use plan — A set of decisions about how the land will be used and ways to achieve the desired use.

It includes the following:
- Definition of goals
- An ordering of land and human and material resources
- An explicit statement of the methods, organization, responsibilities and schedule to be used
- Agreed targets

Line of sight — A general term for the vertical view corridor that might normally be 3° measured up or down from the height of the viewer's eyes.

Local/residential street — Provides access to residences and businesses within a neighborhood

Mixed use development — Development that is created in response to patterns of separate uses that is typical in suburban areas necessitating reliance on cars.

Include residential, commercial, and business accommodations in one area.

No action/No-build policy (do-nothing alternative, null alternative) — A planning option of leaving the situation as it already exists. Existing facilities and services are maintained, and existing transportation policies are continued. Normally includes short-term, minor restoration types of activities (e.g. safety and maintenance improvements) that maintain continuing operation of an existing facility.

Open space

Includes any area of land or water essentially unimproved that is designed or reserved for the purposes similar to the following:
- Preservation of natural resources.
- Managed production of resources.
- Outdoor recreation.
- Protection of public health and safety.
- Farming
- Protection of scenic views and features.
- Environmental protection
- Visual beauty
- Educational opportunities

Open space ratio (OSR) — The proportion of a site that is required to remain as open space and may be used for recreation, agriculture and resource protection.

Ordinance — Formal legislative enactment by the government body of a governing body

Must not be in conflict with any higher form of law to have the full force and effect of law within the boundaries to which it applies.

Ordinance regulations (Typical) — Prevent sediment damage to the storm drain system
- Control storm water discharges to minimize downstream erosion
- Minimize soil exposure
- Establish permanent vegetation

- Stabilize waterways and outlets
- Protect storm water inlets
- Install/maintain ESC facilities and practices

Planned Unit Development (PUD) (Cluster Housing) — A planned unit development (PUD) is a project or subdivision that consists of common property and improvements that are owned and maintained by an owner's association for the benefit and use of the individual units within the project. For a project to qualify as a PUD, the owners' association must require automatic, non-severable membership for each individual unit owner, and provide for mandatory assessments. Zoning is not a basis for classifying a project or subdivision as a PUD.

Police powers — The right of the government to enforce laws for public welfare, including such things as building codes, zoning, etc.

Population density — The number of people in a given area.

Regional land use — Determines how an area is being used and developed and how such use may project into future uses.

Objectives include a spatial distribution of various land uses that:
- Results in a compatible arrangement of land uses
- Protects and uses wisely the region's natural resources including soils, inland lakes and streams, groundwater, wetlands, woodlands, prairies, wildlife, and natural areas and critical species habitats
- Supports transportation, utility and public facility systems
- Does not look at specifics as plant and animal counts

ROW right of way (also right-of-way) — Publicly-owned space for current or future facilities such as highways, streets, or trails, and above and below-ground utilities (like water, sewer, power, and cable.) Generally extends approximately 10' to 20' beyond the curb into the yard area. Privately installed trees, fences, retaining walls, or sprinklers should not be built in the right of way.
- **New Roadway Right of Way**
  - o Dedicated to public use on a subdivision plat
  - o Must be constructed under permit issued by the governing body and comply with the provisions of these regulations during construction in order to be accepted for maintenance
- **Public right-of-way**
  - o Area of real property in which the governing body has a dedicated or acquired right-of-way interest in the real property
  - o Usually includes the area on, below or above the present and future streets, alleys, avenues, roads, highways, parkways or boulevards dedicated or acquired as right-of-way

Setback — Minimum horizontal distance required between any lot line or right-of-way and the nearest point of a building, structure or improvement located or to be located on the lot.

Sight-line triangle — A setback at a street and driveway intersection that restricts anyone from placing view obstructions at the height of the driver's line of sight general located between 3" and 6" above ground for a specified horizontal distance related to street design speed.

Specific area plan — SAP is a legal tool for detailed design and implementation of a defined portion of an area covered by a General Plan. A specific plan may include all detailed regulations, conditions, programs and/or proposed legislation that may be necessary or convenient for the systematic implementation of any General Plan element(s).

Streetscape — Space between the buildings on either side of a street. Includes building frontage/façade; landscaping (trees, yards, bushes, plantings, etc.); sidewalks; street paving; street furniture (benches, kiosks, trash receptacles, fountains, etc.); signs; awnings; and street lighting

Subdivision —Tract of land divided by the owner into blocks, building lots and streets according to a recorded subdivision plat

Subdivision rules and regulations — Procedures, requirements, and provisions governing the subdivision of land that is specified in formal rules and regulations

Sustainable development — Development with the goal of preserving environmental quality, natural resources and livability for present and future generations

Title search or examination — A check of the title records to make sure the buyer is purchasing a house from the legal owner and there are no liens, overdue special assessments, or other claims or outstanding restrictive covenants filed in the record, which would adversely affect the marketability or value of title.

Transfer of development rights — A transfer of development rights allow property owners to sell the development rights to their property while retaining ownership of the land itself. Often used to preserve a natural open space located a large site proposed for residential development.

Variance — Means a modification or waiving of the provisions of code as applied to a specific property

Zoning — Legislative process that classifies land in a community into different areas and districts Regulates building dimensions, density, design, and placement.

Zoning map — A map that defines current zoning designations and land use.

FEDERAL REGULATORY AGENCIES

These agencies set, administer and regulate policies.

Department of the Interior
The Department of the Interior is a federal agency that includes the National Park Service or the Bureau of Land Management. This agency employs more landscape architects than any other federal agency.

Environmental Protection Agency (EPA)
The federal regulatory agency responsible for administering and enforcing federal environmental laws, including the Clean Air Act, the Clean Water Act, the Endangered Species Act, and others.

Army Corp of Engineers
Provides quality, responsive engineering services to the nation including:
- Planning, designing, building and operating water resources and other civil works projects (Navigation, Flood Control, Environmental Protection, Disaster Response, etc.)

Federal Emergency Management Agency (FEMA)
Agency responsible for administering the National Flood Insurance Program

Fish and Wildlife Service
- Provides for wildlife conservation
- Allows for surveys and investigations of wildlife to be conducted in the public domain

FEDERAL ACTS

Federal Water Pollution Act of 1972 (FWPCA) (Clean Water Act)

- Primary federal law in the United States governing water pollution
- Makes it illegal to discharge any toxic or non-toxic pollution without a permit
- Encourages the use of the best available technology for pollution control
- Provides Federal funding for constructing sewage treatment plants

Clean Water Act

- A 1977 amendment to the FWPCA
- Emphasizes the control of toxic pollutants
- Established a program to transfer the responsibility of Federal clean water   programs to the individual states
- Includes dredged materials; solid waste; incinerator residue; sewage; garbage; sewage sludge; munitions; chemical wastes; biological materials; radioactive materials; heat; wrecked or discarded equipment; rock; sand; cellar dirt; and industrial, municipal, and agricultural waste discharged into water (i.e., wastewater, including storm water runoff).

National Pollutant Discharge Elimination System (NPDES)

Permitting system of the Clean Water Act that controls water pollution by regulating point, and nonpoint sources that discharge pollutants into waters of the United States

Endangered Species Act

Governs how animal and plant species whose populations are dangerously in decline or close to extinction will be protected and recovered.

National Environmental Policy Act (NEPA)

Enacted to ensure the integration of natural and social sciences and environmental   design in planning and decision-making for federal projects or projects on federal lands.

Safe Drinking Water Act (SDWA)

- Regulates the treatment of water for human consumption
- Requires testing for and elimination of contaminants for the protection of human health

Watershed Protection and Flood Prevention Act (PL 83-566)

Authorizes states and local agencies to carry out works of improvement for soil conservation and for other purposes including flood prevention; conservation, development, utilization and disposal of water; and conservation and proper utilization of land.

Wellhead Protection Program

- Amendment to the federal Safe Drinking Water Act in 1986
- Minimizes the potential for contamination of public ground water supplies

NATIONAL ORGANIZATIONS

American Institute of Architects (AIA)

- A nationally recognized, professional organization of architects
- Has developed a document entitled "AIA Document A201 - General Conditions of the Contract for Construction ("Document A201")

American Nursery and Landscape Association (ANLA)
- National voice of the nursery and landscape industry
- Sets the standards for acceptable plant health and vigor
- Publishes plant quality standards

American Society for Testing and Materials (ASTM)
Develops technical standards for materials, products, systems, and services
Example: Concrete standards for the United States

American Society of Consulting Arborists (ASCA)
Non-profit professional society created to develop and preserve the highest standards of performance in the field of arboricultural consulting

American Society of Landscape Architects (ASLA)
- National professional association representing landscape architects
- Promotes the landscape architecture profession and advances the practice through advocacy, education, communication, and fellowship
- Governs the use of construction materials throughout North America

Construction Specification Institute (CSI)
- Technical society composed of architects, specifiers, engineers, contractors, product representatives, building owners, and facility managers who create and sustain the built environment
- Provides a common system of organization and presentation of construction information, enhancing communication among all construction industry disciplines

Consumer Product Safety Commission (CPSC)
A federal commission that evaluates products, investigates the causes of product-related injuries, and issues and enforces safety standards.
- Example: Play structure safety and play area surfacing.

Illuminating Engineering Society of North America (IESNA)
Has a Sports and Recreational Areas Lighting Committee
Develops standards and design criteria for various sports, both indoor and outdoor

International Society of Arboriculture
- Worldwide professional organization dedicated to fostering a greater appreciation for trees and to promoting research, technology, and the professional practice of arboriculture.
- Publishes a tree valuation methodology by the Council of Tree and Landscape Appraisers

Leadership in Energy and Environmental Design (LEED)
LEED is a building environmental certification program developed and operated by the U.S. Green Building Council. It is a self-assessing system designed for rating new and existing commercial, institutional, and high-rise residential buildings. It evaluates environmental performance from a "whole building" perspective over a building's life cycle, providing a definitive standard for what constitutes a green building.
Points are awarded for credits achieved, with a total of 69 points possible. Forty percent of these points must be achieved to gain certification, which includes four progressive levels: Certified,

Silver, Gold and Platinum with platinum being the highest and most honorable. To earn the designation, buildings must earn points in the categories of sustainable sites, water efficiency, energy and atmosphere, materials and resources, indoor environmental air quality, and innovation and design process.

Landscape Contractors Association (LCA)
An association that exists to provide local resources to landscape professionals to help them maximize their business potentials.

National Evaluation Service(NES)
An arm of the Council of American Building Officials sponsored jointly by the three major American model code organizations - the International Conference of Building Officials (ICBO); the Southern Building Code Congress International (SBCCI); and the Building Officials and Code Administrators International (BOCA). NES studies applications for new products, and publishes evaluation reports recommending approval by its three constituent members.

STATE, REGIONAL, AND LOCAL RESPONSIBILITIES

State
- Adopt laws that establish policy and regulatory frameworks for governmental guidance of development and conservation
- Provide direction to local governments about the content of and process for adopting a land use plan
- Authorize local governments to control the location and nature of development (Generally)
- Erect new legal and institutional structures that integrate state, regional, and local guidance of developments and conservation of natural resources such as coastal zone management
- Establish comprehensive state goals and policy priorities for community development and institute new intergovernmental procedures for achieving those goals and priorities

Regional
Composed of geographic region
- Subject to state rules for special district (like local water district)
- Has authority to set rules for issues of "regional significance"
- Required to plan and to coordinate local plans
- May review developments that have regional impacts, thus linking the agencies directly with the development process
- Allow regionalized concentration of staff, services, equipment, and materials to provide a cost-effective mechanism to meet federal and state obligations
- May apply sanctions

Local
- Provide government services more efficiently and responsively than could be done by the state
- Control own planning and decision making
- Include police power to enforce land use plans and zoning
- Allow for transfer of development rights
- Comply with regional issues
- Establish statutes that spell out the elements of local comprehensive plans

Site Design

Following the site analysis, a developmental plan is created to cause the least amount of disruption to a site and to avoid critical areas.

SITE DESIGN CONSIDERATIONS

Decreasing impervious surfaces helps to avoid problems from storm water runoff and water table depletion, by reducing surfaces that prevent natural filtration.

Methods may include:

Reducing Roadway Surfaces
Retains more permeable land area
- Examples: Shared driveway, landscaped detention islands within cul-de-sacs

Permeable Pavement Surfaces
- Areas allow water to flow through, replenishing soil areas directly beneath
- Constructed from a variety of materials, including traditional asphalt and concrete, gravel or pavers with sub-base engineered to accommodate temporary water storage and filtration
- May reduce or eliminate the need for traditional storm water structures

Planning site layout and grading to natural land contours
- Retain or enhance contours and incorporated into the landscaping design.
- Minimizes grading costs
- Retains a greater percentage of the land's natural hydrology which functions as filtration basins

Natural Resource Preservation
Used to minimize the need for irrigation systems
- Examples: Stream bank (in most areas, subject to Federal or State regulations)

Xeriscaping
- Refers to landscaping with plants native to area climate and soil conditions
- Requires less maintenance and irrigation than most hybrid or imported varieties

Clustering Homes
- Occurs on slightly smaller lot areas
- Can allow more preserved open space to be used for recreation, visual aesthetics, and wildlife habitat
- Can reduce infrastructure costs to the builder, since fewer feet of pipe, cable, and pavement are needed, and maintenance costs are reduced for homeowners

Code/Regulatory
Federal, state, local and subdivision statutes mandating the implementation of storm water management plans.

MAPS

Zoning map
- Divides a city into areas according to use
- Used to control growth and population densities
  - Example: Single-family residences, industrial plants

Quadrangle map
- Used to show structures, topography, water and roadways

Assessor's map
- Used to locate buildings and land in order to determine their value

City master plan map
- Used to show how a city may be developed over a long period of time
- Allows for an area to be rezone
- Example: Old warehouse district being turned into residential housing.

SITE SELECTION

A carefully selected site will save work, expense, materials, and repairs.

Slope
- Provide the best views and offer advantages in water and air drainage. Excavating a flat pad on a sloped site can provide earth for building, gardening, or landscaping.
- Very steep slopes (over 8%) require excessive digging and may be difficult to get around on during building.

Aspect
- Direction a sloped site faces affects ground temperature
- South-facing slopes tend to collect more heat in the winter, which contributes to energy savings.

Drainage
- Avoid marshy areas, flood plains, and depressions.
- Stay away from seasonal creeks and gullies where surface water may flow only during part of the year or only once every several years.
- Determine where the water would flow
- Put the building on a slope so that you can create artificial drainage if site has a poorly drained clay soil and a rainy climate. High water table means there will be drainage problems and possibly wetland conflicts.

Subsurface Geology
- How far down it is to bedrock
- How much topsoil there is
- What kinds of amendments the soil needs for building with.
- Whether the site is seismically stable

Microclimate

- **Solar Access**
  - Where winter heating is needed, windows on the south side (or an attached greenhouse) make a big difference.
  - Unobstructed view to the horizon from the southeast to the southwest provide best sites for passive solar heating (and for photovoltaic electricity).
- **Shade**
  - Hot summer climates benefit from afternoon shading.
  - Plan for tall trees on the southwest and west of the site.
  - Deciduous trees block the summer sun but drop their leaves and let the winter sun through. Trees/vegetation around a site tend to keep it cooler and moister.
- **Prevailing Wind Direction**
  - Because of local topography (valley, ridge, water), wind direction on a specific site can vary enormously from the regional norm.
  - Determine the direction of the biggest storms approach site.
- **Air Drainage**
  - On clear winter nights, air cools off and condenses wherever it is exposed to the sky, flowing downhill. Wherever its passage is blocked by a rise in the ground, a line of trees, or even a building, it comes to rest, creating 'frost pockets' of much colder air. These are the places that freeze first.
  - Position buildings so air can drain away and where early morning winter sun will warm them up sooner

BUILDING PLACEMENT CHARACTERISTICS

- Minimize storm water runoff
- Minimize habitat disturbance
- Protect open space
- Reduce the risk of erosion
- Save energy by providing for passive solar, natural ventilation, and day lighting.

SUBDIVISION PLAT

- Proposed streets are properly oriented and integrated with existing streets and are of adequate width.
- Street intersections are safe and avoid dog-legs that create dangerous jogs.
- Lots satisfy area and other dimensional requirements of the zoning code.
- Lot layout is sound.
- Sites dedicated or reserved for parks, or for other public facilities such as schools
- Utility easements, such as those for electricity, gas, phone, cable
- Storm water detention or retention facilities provided
- Sewer lines
- Water lines
- Thoroughfares
- Sidewalks throughout the subdivision connect with other sidewalks in the area
- Traffic calming methods are used to move traffic through residential neighborhoods via raised intersections, differing pavement textures, shifts in direction, grassy road shoulders, narrowed travel ways, "street trees," roundabouts, medians

HOUSING TYPES

Cluster housing

Allows units to be clustered on a usable part of a site to avoid unbuildable sensitive portions of the site, like wetlands, streams, and their buffers. Not limited in size but generally sit on a small lot size for owners who do not want a large yard.

Cottage housing

Grouping of small, single family dwelling units clustered around a common area and developed with a coherent plan for the entire site

Cul-de-sac

A street which meets another street at one end but is closed at the other, such that little traffic will travel down it and the property owners enjoy excellent privacy. Also, this widens sufficiently at the end to permit an automobile to make a "U" turn

Single family housing

- Overwhelming preference in the United States
- Surveys by Fannie Mae indicate that upwards of 85% of Americans would prefer to live in a detached house, and that they will make major sacrifices to do so.
- Residents place a very high value on safety, quiet and privacy, a large yard three important features of single family, detached housing in low density neighborhoods.

SITE FURNISHINGS

Site furnishings include utilitarian outdoor manmade amenities that are needed to service the needs of the public and/or that assist in the safe and orderly management of the site. Items include picnic table, benches, tables, bike racks and trash receptacles. Site furnishing can be classified as

- **Hardscape**
  - Refers to the inanimate (i.e., non-living) elements of a landscape
  - Composed of concrete, brick or stone, in addition to wood
- **Softscape**
  - Living plants

NEEDS ASSESSMENT

Analysis conducted by the designer in initial stages of design to determine client's landscaping needs and interests.

SITE ANALYSIS

The purpose of the analysis is to provide thorough information about the site assets and liabilities prior to starting the design process in order to develop concepts that incorporate meaningful responses to the external conditions of the site.

Typical site information includes the following:

- Topography, slope, and adjacent landforms
- Soil types, textures, and load-bearing capacity
- Vegetative cover and existing native plant populations
- Geologic and seismic data
- Parcel shape and access with adjacent land uses, buildings and structures
- Utility easements or corridors
- Utility lines and sizes
- Road system and networks for parking, pedestrians, bicycles, and transit
- Security and safety improvements
- Microclimate factors (e.g., solar and wind loads)
- Proposed future development
- Shape, massing, materials, structural systems, mechanical systems, access and service, solar orientation, and provisions for security and fire safety

ENVIRONMENTAL SITE ASSESSMENT

It involves researching historical use of property and visually inspecting the property for signs of activity that may have caused a release of a hazardous substance. Although not required by law, an environmental professional is generally retained to perform this investigation.

- Determine if any environmental issue exists at the subject parcels.
- Identify property development and former land use from available aerial photographs, historical documents
- Determine if underground storage tanks are located at the subject parcels, or if any other environmental issues exist at the parcels. City Fire Marshal files are often much more extensive than the State Fire Marshal files (which should also be reviewed).
- Determine if environmental issues (potential sources of contamination) exist at the subject parcels.
- Report documentations (conclusions recommendations)

BASE INFORMATION

Record base information in the form of a site location map (small-scale) and a site topographic map (larger scale)

Site Location Map
Small-scale map showing the general location of the project with respect to nearby features such as water bodies, structures, roads, and utilities.

Site Topographic Map
- Records existing topographic contours, drainage, general vegetative cover types (e.g. grass, forest, field), streams, ponds, wetlands, undisturbed riparian buffers, utilities, existing roads and buildings, and accurate property lines.
- Records the soil types and slopes on the site

SOILS INFORMATION
Evaluate soil types and erodabilities to make erosion control suggestions
Soil types
- **Loamy soils** (loam and sandy loam textures)
- **Clayey soils** (clay, clay loam, silty clay loam, or sandy clay loam)
- **Silty Soils** (silt and silt loam texture)

Erodabilities factors
- Soil texture
- Organic matter content
- Soil structure
- Permeability (the rate at which water can move through the soil). .

EROSION POTENTAL CAUSES

- Nearby waterways or bodies of water
- Highly or moderately erodable soils
- Slopes with high or medium erosion potential
- Absence of well-vegetated areas
- Duration of exposure
- Slopes
  Low (0 to 8%)
  Medium (8 to 16%)
  High (over 16%) erosion potential

VEGETATION

Survey
- Record existing vegetation
- Label individual large trees by diameter at breast height in inches
  - Example – 42" sugar maple.
- Try to save large specimen trees when planning layout of the development. If any grading must be done under the dripline (canopy) of the tree, however, the tree is less likely to survive

Classification of Vegetation
- Softwood (evergreen)
- Mixed softwood and hardwood
- Hardwood
- Old field, pasture, etc.

Soil

Soil is defined as the unconsolidated mineral and organic material on the immediate surface of the earth that serves as a natural medium for the growth of land plants

COMPOSITION

- Soil is made up of solids, liquids and gases. For growing plants, each phase is essential for their life and growth.
    - **Solid** is the mineral (non-living or inorganic) material and the living (organic) matter components.
    - **Liquid** is the water
    - **Gas** is oxygen and others.
- The amounts of each type of matter in the soil determine the type of soil as classified by scientists.
    - Example: Organic soils found in bogs and wetlands are composed of at least 20% organic matter

THREE BASIC SOIL GROUPS

Cohesive soils

Have the smallest particles.
- Includes clay (particle size range of .00004" to .002") which is used in embankment fills and retaining pond beds
- Includes silt which ranges from .0002" to .003".
- Plastic when wet
- Can be molded, but become very hard when dry. .
- Usually require a force such as impact or pressure.

Granular soils
- Range in particle size from .003" to .08" (sand) and .08" to 1.0" (fine to medium gravel).
- Known for their water-draining properties
- Obtain maximum density in either a fully dry or saturated state.

Organic
- Not suitable for compaction

SOIL CONSISTENCY TERMS

Refers to the soil's response to stress
Cemented
- Hard; little affected by moistening
Firm
- When moist, crushes under moderate pressure between thumb and forefinger, but resistance is distinctly noticeable

Friable
- When moist, crushes easily under gentle pressure between thumb and forefinger and can be pressed together into a lump

Hard
- When dry, moderately resistant to pressure; can be broken with difficulty between thumb and forefinger

Loose
- Noncoherent when dry or moist; does not hold together in a mass

Plastic
- When wet, readily deformed by moderate pressure but can be pressed into a lump; will form a "wire" when rolled between thumb and forefinger.

Sticky
- When wet, adheres to other material and tends to stretch somewhat and pull apart rather than to pull free from other material

Soft
- When dry, breaks into powder or single grains under very slight pressure.

TEXTURE

- Term commonly used to designate the proportionate distribution of the different sizes of mineral particles in a soil
- The USDA Soil texture classes are sand, loamy sands, sandy loams, loam, silt loam, silt, sandy clay loam, clay loam, silty clay loam, sandy clay, silty clay, and clay.

SOIL TRIANGLE

Any three percentages of sand, silt, and clay that add up to 100 will always define a single point on the triangle. Example: **Loam** is soil that is 7 to 27% clay, 28 to 50% silt, and less than 52% sand

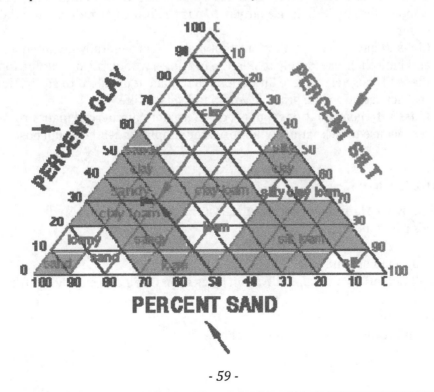

PERMEABILITY

The quality of the soil that enables water to move downward through the profile
Permeability is measured as the number of inches per hour that water moves downward through the saturated soil. Terms describing permeability are:

Very slow	less than 0.06 inch/hr
Slow	0.06 to 0.2 inch/hr
Moderately slow	0.2 to 0.6 inch/hr
Moderate	0.6 inch to 2.0 inches/hr
Moderately rapid	0.0 to 6.0 inches/hr
Rapid	6.0 to 20 inches/hr
Very rapid	more than 20 inches/hr

LAND CAPABILITY CLASS

These eight land capability classes are distinguished according to the risk of land damage or the difficulty of land use.

- **Land suitable for cultivation and other uses**
  - **Class I** has few limitations that restrict their use.
  - **Class II** has some limitations that reduce the choice of plants or require moderate conservation practices.
  - **Class III** has severe limitations that reduce the choice of plants or require special conservation practices, or both.
  - **Class IV** has very severe limitations that restrict the choice of plants, require very careful management, or both.

- **Land generally not suitable for cultivation (without major treatment)**
  - **Class V** have little or no erosion hazard but have other limitations, impractical to remove, that limit their use largely to pasture, range, woodland, or wildlife food and cover.
  - **Class VI** have severe limitations that make them generally unsuited for cultivation and limit their use largely to pasture or range, woodland, or wildlife food and cover.
  - **Class VII** has very severe limitations that make it unsuited to cultivation and that restrict use largely to grazing, woodland, or wildlife.
  - **Class VIII** has limitations that preclude use for commercial plant production and restrict use to recreation, wildlife, water supply, or aesthetic purpose

HYDROLIC SOIL GROUPS

Soils are classified by the Natural Resource Conservation Service into four Hydrologic Soil Groups based on the soil's runoff potential.
Group A
- Sand, loamy sand or sandy loam types of soils
- Low runoff potential and high infiltration rates even when thoroughly wetted
Group B
- Silt loam or loam
- Moderate infiltration rate when thoroughly wetted

Group C

- Sandy clay loam
- Low infiltration rates when thoroughly wetted

Group D

- Clay loam, silty clay loam, sandy clay, silty clay or clay
- Highest runoff potential

CONCEPTS

Aerobic — The ability of organisms or tissues to function only with the presence of free oxygen.

Alluvial — A general term for the sediments laid down in river beds, floodplains, lakes, fans at the foot of the mountain slopes and estuaries during relatively recent geologic times.

Anaerobic Soil — Soil that is devoid of interstitial oxygen. In wetlands this condition most normally occurs because of the sustained presence of water, which limits contact with the atmosphere.

Angle of Repose — The angle between the horizontal and the maximum slope that a soil assumes through natural processes.

Bearing capacity (Soil capacity) — A measure of the load per unit area that a material can withstand before failure. This is an important feature when determining the sizing of a footing.

Compressive Strength — Resistance to a crushing or buckling force, the maximum compressive load a specimen sustains divided by its original cross-sectional area.

Cubic yard — A volume measure commonly applied to rock or soil material. One cubic yard is a cube of material that measures one yard in length, width, and height. One cubic-yard equals 27 cubic-feet.

Hydric Soil — A type of soil with characteristics resulting from prolonged saturation and chemically reducing conditions that occurs under anaerobic conditions.

Liquefaction — The point at which soil acts like a liquid, typically under earthquake conditions.

Loam — Mixture of two or more soil ingredients

Mineral Soil — Having properties determined predominantly by mineral matter. Usually contains less than 20% organic matter.

Organic matter — Plant and animal residue in the soil at various stages of decomposition. This is a good source of nitrogen and other nutrients for crops.

Percolation — Movement of water through a porous substance, as through soils of a spreading basin.

Shear strength — The ability of a soil to hold together under pressure from a downhill force.

SLOPE

Slope is important to soil formation and management because of its influence on runoff, soil drainage, erosion, use of machinery, and choice of vegetation.

Slope

- Incline or gradient of a surface and is commonly expressed in percent.
- Determined by measuring the difference in vertical elevation in feet over 100' of horizontal distance.
    o Example: A 5% slope rises or falls 5' per 100' of horizontal distance.

Simple slope
- Has a smooth appearance with surfaces extending in one or perhaps two directions.
- Greater than 1% should only be irrigated with sprinkler or drip systems.
- 1% or less are commonly used for gravity (surface) irrigation
- Example: Foot slopes of river valleys

Complex slope
- Have short slopes which extend in several directions
- Consist of convex and concave slopes
- Example: Knoll
- Greater than 1% should only be irrigated with sprinkler or drip systems.

Shape
- **Convex slope** curves outward like the outside surface of a ball
- **Concave slope** curves inward like the inside surface of a saucer
- **Plane slope** is like a tilted flat surface.

EROSION

A group of processes whereby earth or rock material is loosened or dissolved and removed from any part of the earth's surface. Generally caused by heavy down pours of rain, water in general, snow and ice, wind, harsh chemicals, or even builders or contractors.

Erosion control methods
- **Erosion Control Blankets** are made up of straw or synthetic materials.
  - Helps contain extremely erosive soil where vegetation is planted.
  - These are very sturdy and can last for several years.
- **Riprap** is heavy stone placed around inlets and outlets of pipes or paved channels to provide protection against erosion.
  - Permanent, erosion-resistant protective layer intended to prevent soil erosion in areas of concentrated flow, turbulence or wave energy.
- **Fiber roll product** protects the bank by stabilizing the toe of the slope and by trapping sediment from the sloughing bank. Used where portions of the bank are bare and other parts are stabilized by existing vegetation
- A **perimeter diversion dike** is a dike or dike and channel constructed along the perimeter of a disturbed construction area.
- A **temporary right-of-way** (roadway) diversion is a ridge of compacted soil, loose rock or gravel placed perpendicular to roads, disturbed right-of-ways or similar long sloping areas that are disturbed
- A **water bar** is a permanent ridge or ridge and channel constructed diagonally across a sloping road, utility right-of-way, or path that is subject to erosion

Erosion factor K
- Indicates the susceptibility of a soil to sheet and rill erosion by water
- Values of K range from 0.05 to 0.69.
- The higher the value, the more susceptible the soil is to erosion by water.

Erosion factor T

- An estimate of the maximum average annual rate of soil erosion by wind or water that can occur without affecting productivity over a sustained period.
- The rate is in tons per acre per year.

Erodibility index (EI)

- A numerical expression of the potential of a soil to erode.
- The higher the index, the greater the risk for erosion.
- EI scores of 8 or above are equated to highly erodible land.

ERODABILITY

Erodability depends on such soil characteristics as the content of sand, silt, and clay (soil texture); organic matter content; soil structure; and soil permeability (the rate at which water can move through the soil).

Erodability ratings

- Low erodability.23 and lower
- Moderate erodability.26 to .36
- High erodability.37 and higher

Loamy soils (loam and sandy loam textures)

- Classified as moderately erodable
- Easier to dig than clay soils when dry
- Does not produce as much sediment as clayey soils

Clayey soils (clay, clay loam, silty clay loam, or sandy clay loam)

- Classified as moderately erodable
- Usually difficult to dig when dry
- May form rills on slopes after a hard rain with a large amount of sediment collecting at the base of slopes
- Easily transportable but harder to detach than silty soils
- Can cause serious sedimentation problems because they stay in suspension in water longer
- Harder to catch in sediment basins.

Silty Soils (silt and silt loam texture)

- Very highly erodable
- Particles are easily detached by rainfall and transported by runoff.
- Powdery when dry
- Does not stick together when moist.
- Rills and shallow channels on slopes after a hard rain with large amounts of sediment accumulating at the base of slopes.

Soil Classification Systems

Most soil classification systems used in construction classify soils based upon two experimental characterizations of soil. These two measurements are a grain-size distribution curve (or gradation curve).

MEASUREMENT SYSTEMS

Grain size distribution of the particles
- **Coarse grained soils**
  - Grains large enough to be seen
- **Gravel**
  - Can be picked up with thumb and forefinger
- **Sand**
  - Particles large enough to be seen but too small to be picked up individually
  - Coarse soil with little or no fine particles (5 mm to 0.010 mm)
- **Fine grained soils**
  - Grains too small to be seen
  - Cohesive in nature
  - Tends to compress
- **Silt**
  - Finer than sands, but coarser than clays
  - Slightly finer material is classified as (0.010 mm to 0.005 mm)
- **Clay**
  - Consist of microscopic flake-shaped crystalline minerals
  - Plate-shaped
  - Finer than 0.005 mm
  - Expands with moisture causing problems in foundations

Plastic limit
- Moisture content in the soil at the threshold between semi-solid and plastic
- Determined by rolling a thread of soil on a glass plate until the 1/8" -diameter thread begins to crumble
- Explained in ASTM procedure D-4318

Liquid limit
- Moisture content in the soil at the threshold between plastic and liquid
- Determined by forming a groove in a dish of soil and impacting the dish until the groove closes
- Conducted following the ASTM procedure D-4318
- Large liquid limit indicates high compressibility and high shrink swell tendencies

Shrinkage limit
- Water content, expressed as a percentage of the weight of the oven-dried soil, at which further loss in moisture will not cause a decrease in its volume

MOST WIDELY USED CLASSIFCATION SYSTEMS

Unified Soil Classification System (USCS)
- Most widely used and accepted classification system
- Classifies soils according to properties that affect their use as construction material
- Classified according to:
  o Grain-size distribution of the fraction less than 3" in diameter
  o Plasticity index
  o Liquid limit
  o Organic matter content

- Unified system assumes that
  o Course material is better than fines
  o Low liquid limit is better than high
  o Narrow range from the plastic limit to the liquid limit is better than a wide range
  o Well graded material is better than poorly graded material
    ▪ **Well graded** means lots of sizes mixed together which allows small materials to fill the pores between larger materials and give a denser mix than does uniformly sized materials

- Following group symbols are used in USCS
  G Gravel
  S Sand
  M Silt
  C Clay
  O Organic
  PT Peat
  W Well graded
  P Poorly graded
  L Low liquid limit compressibility; lean (clay)
     Low liquid limit; (silts); plasticity
  H High liquid limit, compressibility; fat (clays)
     High liquid limit; elastic (silts)

AASHTO classification system
American Association of State Highway Officials classification system identifies soils based on their suitability for highway subgrade use.

Group A
- Has a high infiltration rate (low runoff potential) when thoroughly wet
- Consists mainly of deep, well drained to excessively drained sands or gravelly sands

Group B
- Has a moderate infiltration rate when thoroughly wet
- Consists chiefly of moderately deep or deep, moderately well drained or well drained soils that have moderately fine texture to moderately coarse texture

Group C
- Has a slow infiltration rate when thoroughly wet
- Consists chiefly of soils having a layer that impedes the downward movement of water or soils of moderately fine texture or fine texture

Group D
- Has a very slow infiltration rate (high runoff potential) when thoroughly wet.
- Consists chiefly of
  - Clays that have a high shrink-swell potential
  - Soils that have a permanent high water table
  - Soils that have a claypan or clay layer at or near the surface
  - Soils that are shallow over nearly impervious material

Soil Compaction

Soil compaction is defined as the method of mechanically increasing the density of soil by reducing the total pore space in a soil. Almost all types of building sites and construction projects utilize mechanical compaction techniques.

PURPOSE

- Increases load-bearing capacity
- Prevents soil settlement and frost damage
- Provides stability
- Reduces water seepage, swelling and contraction
- Reduces settling of soil

PRINCIPLE TYPES OF COMPACTION FORCE

Static
- Deadweight of the machine, applying downward force on the soil surface, compressing the soil particles
- May be changed by adding or subtracting the weight of the machine
- Confined to upper soil layers
- Examples: Kneading and pressure

Vibratory
- Uses a mechanism, usually engine-driven, to create a downward force in addition to the machine's static weight
- Use a certain amount of force to overcome the cohesive nature of particular particles
- Examples: rammers and compactors

TYPES OF TESTS

A particular soil needs to have an ideal (or optimum) amount of moisture to achieve maximum density. This is important not only for durability, but will save money because less compaction effort is needed to achieve the desired results.

Proctor Test
- Determines the maximum density of a soil needed for a specific job site
- Tests the effects of moisture on soil density
- Expresses value as a percentage of density which is determined before any compaction takes place to develop the compaction specifications.
- Modified Proctor values are higher because they take into account higher densities needed for certain typed of construction projects.
- Test methods are similar for both tests.

Modified Method (Modified Proctor Test)
- Uses the equivalent energy or compactive effort of 64,439 ft.-lbs./sq. ft./1 ft. layer
- Requires 4.5 times more effort than required by the Standard Compaction method
- Required where foundations are to be placed in the soil backfill, and where minimal or no settlement can be tolerated by the structure

Field Test
Used to know and control the soil density during compaction.
- **The Hand Test**
  - Pick up a handful of soil, squeeze and open.
  - If the soil is moldable and breaks into only a couple of pieces when dropped, it has the right amount of moisture for proper compaction.
- **Sand Cone Test**
  - Compares density of the soil that was just compacted to the density obtained from the Proctor test of soil from the same area.
- **Nuclear Density**
  - Uses a radioactive isotope source (Cesium 137) at the soil surface (backscatter) from a probe placed into the soil (direct transmission)
  - Gives off photons (usually Gamma rays) which radiate back to the meter's detectors on the bottom of the unit
  - Dense soil absorbs more radiation than loose soil and the readings reflect overall density.
- **Soil Modulus (soil stiffness)**
  - **Soil stiffness** is the ratio of force-to-displacement
  - Desired engineering property
  - Machine sends vibrations into the soil and then measures the deflection of the soil from the vibrations
  - Very recent development that replaces soil density testing

STRESS

Stress refers to pressure/force/weight that is applied to the soil

Compressive stress
- A force that tends to compress the surface

Tensional stress
- The opposite of compressional stress; occurs when one part moves away from another part that does not move

Strain
- The response to stress

Yield point
- Point at which a material fails (deformability and firmness of a soil)
- Often plotted as a function of stress by engineers

GRADING

Grade
- The level or the surface of the ground established by law or on record where not established by law

Exterior Surface Grading
- Designed to direct surface water away from or around the home
- Avoids water penetration problems such as
  - Structural damage to wood framing
  - Interior damage
  - Hydrostatic pressure against foundation walls
  - Cracking of the slab and foundation walls

Grading of the Soil around the Perimeter of the Home
- Slope away (at a minimum rate of 1" per foot for the first 6') from the house to prevent rain water from accumulating next to the foundation
- Refers to the layer of soil that is impervious to water such as clay, which directs the water away from the house
  - Topsoil is porous (as would be used for planting) and absorbs the surface water
  - Sub-layer of clay or similar non-porous soil prevents the water from continuing in a downward movement and directs the water laterally

Grading of the Lot
- Directs water around and away from the house to avoid receiving water run-off
- Create swales (shallow ditches) to direct the water around the house

RESIDENTIAL EXCAVATIONS

- Usually type C soil
- Will require slope at 1½:1
- The soils pile is at least 2' back from the edge of the excavation

Section 3: Design

Elements of Design

The elements of design refer to form, line, plane, volume, shape, scale, pattern, texture and color.

FORM

Basic shape or contour of an object or space

Form vocabulary
- Cylindrical
- Flat
- Square

How form is perceived
- Lines
- Planes
- Volume
- Point

Factors that affect form
- Light
- Color
- Human perception

LINE

A continuous mark whose length is greater than its width

Line vocabulary
- Horizontal
- Vertical
- Diagonal
- Curved

How line is perceived
- **Horizontal**
  - Suggests restfulness, stability
  - Creates an illusion of lesser height by creating the impression of movement around the site by using horizontals like a row of chairs, plants
- **Vertical**
  - Suggests strength, equilibrium, permanence and a strong upward movement
  - Creates an illusion of higher height with tall plants and columns that take eye upwards

- **Diagonal**
    - Suggests power
    - Represents movement either upward or downward
    - Can create an illusion of imbalance

- **Curved**
    - Suggest graceful and gentle movements
    - Can be either geometric or free form

How line is created
- When actual length greatly exceeds actual width
- When one plane meets another
- When there is a change in material, texture or color

How line is introduced into a space
- Addition of objects with dynamic linear form
- Inclusion of linear structural elements
- Utilization of applied decorations and finish materials
- Selection of lightning

Architectural features principle
- Use the strongest lines already in the room

PLANE

Surface enclosed by the two dimensions of length and width (ceiling or wall)

Purpose of plane
- Defines space
- Determines the character of a space by adding texture, color and pattern

How plane is utilized in a space
- By treating a single surface with only one color and texture
- By subdividing surface with varying materials, textures, and colors
- By harmonizing or contrasting design elements such as furniture and accessories

VOLUME

Three-dimensional object or space that has length, width, and depth

Volume concepts
- **Positive or solid**
    - Three-dimensional object or space that has length, width, and depth
- **Negative or void**
    - Empty space
- **Regular**
    - Volume with a definite such as a square

- **Irregular**
  Free-formed shapes such as a tree
- **Dominant**
  o Prominent characteristic such as tall or crescent shape

SHAPE

Form of an object or space that differentiates it from other objects or spaces

Shape vocabulary
- **Geometric** (circle)
  o **Circle** (completeness)
  o **Square** (stability)
- **Irregular** (broken glass)
- **Natural** (shrub)
- **Combined**

SCALE

Comparison of the size of an object as it relates to another object of known size
- **Judgment of scale**
  o In relation to humans either directly or indirectly
  o In relation to nonhuman objects such as doors and windows to walls
- **Purpose of scale**
  o Create feeling such as intimacy
  o Integrate diverse forms through emphasis or contrast
- No set rules for scale relationships
- Human scale is the most commonly used scale

COLOR

Refers to a visual perception of light casting on objects in various hues, lightness and/or saturation

Color terms
Hue - Basic colors such as red, yellow, blue, or green
Value - Degree of lightness or darkness of a color in relation to white and black
Intensity or **chroma** - Purity of a color
Tint - Created when white is added to a hue
Shade - Created when black is added
Tone - Created when gray or its complement is added

Complementary - Located opposite each other on the color wheel

- Example: Blue is the complement of orange.
  - o Reinforce each other
  - o Can create an afterimage of its complement
  - o Can induce its complement in the background
  - o Will heighten its complement when side by side
  - o Will intensify the smaller complement when backed by the larger complement

Noncomplementary
- Creates an illusion of tint by its complement when side by side
- Creates an illusion distance
- Will be absorbed by a background color

Primary colors - Red, yellow and blue
- Third primary will tint the other two when used together.

Simultaneous contrast
- Light color appears lighter against a darker color.
- Darker color appears darker against a lighter color.

Cool colors - Blue, green and violet
- Suggests peace, quiet, nature, cool, calming
- Causes objects to recede

Warm colors - Red, yellow and orange
- Suggests excitement, heat, activeness,
- Causes objects to advance

5 color schemes
- **Monochromatic**
  - o Composed of tints and shades in a single hue
  - o Uses shades of same color
  - o Can be the most monotonous
- **Analogous**
  - o Uses hues that are close to each other on the color wheel
  - o Uses primary, secondary, and tertiary colors
  - o Most effective when one color is dominant
- **Complementary**
  - o Use of colors on the opposite sides of the color wheel
    - ❖ **Split complementary**
      - ▪ Uses a color on one side of the color wheel
      - ▪ Uses the two colors that lie on either side of the complementary color
    - ❖ **Double complementary**
      - ▪ Uses 4 colors
      - ▪ Consists of a pair on either side of the two complements
      - ▪ Most effective when one color is dominant

- **Triad**
  - Uses a range 3 of colors that are equally spaced around the color wheel
  - Uses combinations such as blue to green, red to violet, and yellow to orange
  - Most effective when one color is dominant
- **Tetrad**
  - Uses four colors that are equally spaced around the color wheel
  - Most effective when one or two colors are dominant

TEXTURE

Feel and look of different surfaces

Types
- **Actual texture**
  - Physical feel of a surface such as the roughness as of bricks
- **Visual texture**
  - Acquired knowledge of how different surfaces feel such as sod and concrete

How texture is perceived
- Closeness emphasizes texture
- Distance diminishes texture

How texture is used
- Adds interest
- Enhances the design concept
- Accentuates various design objects
- Regulates light
- Adds balance
- Creates a theme
- Affects spatial perception
- Defines a focal point

Effects of light on texture
- Minimizes with diffuse, strong and direct light
- Emphasizes with strong side lighting
- Creates glare on smooth glossy surfaces
- Shows imperfections
- Reduces brightness and color

PATTERN

Repetitious arrangement of design or decoration

Types of pattern
- Two dimensional
- Linear

How it is created
- Built in
- Applied

How pattern is used
- Adds interest
- Enhances the design concept
- Accentuates various design objects
- Regulates light
- Adds balance
- Creates a theme
- Affects spatial perception
- Defines a focal point

Principles of Design

The **principles of design** refer to balance, emphasis, movement, pattern, proportion, repetition, rhythm, variety, and unity.

BALANCE

Arrangement of objects around an imaginary central point to achieve a pleasing result

Types
- **Formal Balance**
  - All elements centered within the layout.
  - Creates a restrained, conservative look
  - Good choice for designs that must imply dignity, strength, and dependability
- **Informal Balance**
  - Offers a greater range of positioning your elements
  - Can use elements of different size, shapes, and contrast
  - Can also vary their positions relative to the center of the layout
  - Creates a more casual relaxed feel in design
  - Can stimulate interest and generate excitement.
  - Can create eye-flow that leads through the layout along the path you specify.

Balance variables
- **Heaviness**
  - Large objects when compared with smaller objects with the same design elements.
  - Created by dark, highly textured, and highly detailed elements
- **Weight**
  - Bright color when compared to neutral colors
  - Complex or unusual shapes when compared with simple shapes
- **Number**
  - Single object can be balanced with several small objects
- **Imaginary vertical axis**
  - Conceived point in which design elements are balanced

Three types of balance
- **Symmetrical (bisymmetrical, bilateral, axial)**
  - Centering identical objects on a central point to be aesthetically pleasing to the eye (bisymmetrical, bilateral, axial)
    - Can be concrete or abstract axis
    - Can be centered or off centered
  - Suggests formality, stability
  - Characterizes traditional designs
  - Used with other balance concepts.
- **Asymmetrical**
  - Centers unequal objects on a central point to be aesthetically pleasing to the eye
  - Described as **informal** and **dynamic**
  - Effective in combining different objects, forms, colors and textures into a cohesive unit.
  - Created by the designer "eye" as no fixed rules

- **Radial**
  - o Centering objects in a circular pattern around a central point to be aesthetically pleasing to the eye
    - ▪ Example: Circular patio table surrounded by identical chairs, equally spaced
  - o Directs eye on the center of the grouping

HARMONY AND UNITY

Harmony
- An agreeable arrangement of individual objects sharing a common characteristic to be aesthetically pleasing to the eye
  - o Example: Grouping objects that share the same scale, form or color

Unity
- An ordering of all elements in a design project so that each contributes to a unified aesthetic effect.

Achieved by
- Combining a number of design elements (plants) that may share similar design elements such as scale, form and color
- Arranging design elements in close proximity
- Coordinating them to a common architectural detail
- Arranging design items around a shared design feature
- Using variety of design elements to avoid monotony

RHYTHM

Created
- When one or more design elements are used repeatedly to create a feeling of organized movement

Types of rhythm
- **Repetition**
  - o Uniform repetition
  - o Irregular spacing
  - o Focusing or changing design objects at regular intervals
- **Gradation**
  - o Modify design by increasing or decreasing size.
  - o Modify design by changing color, shapes, forms, textures and various design objects
- **Pattern**
  - o Repeating of an object or symbol all over the artwork

EMPHASIS AND FOCUS

Emphasis
- Making selected design element(s) more noticeable than its surroundings
  - Example: View

Focal point
- Specific visual elements such as a spectacular view, fireplace, art, sculpture or furniture piece, which becomes the main focus of the problem.
- Hierarchy of space
  - **Dominant**: Main area of focus
  - **Subordinate**: Secondary area of focus

Movement
- Path the viewer's eye takes through the artwork, often to focal areas
- Can be directed along lines edges, shape and color within the artwork

How to create
- By location
- Centered
- Off-centered
- At the end of an axis
- By design elements ((size, color, shape, texture)
- By creating a marked contrast

CONTRAST AND VARIETY

Contrast
- Use of opposite design elements as color, form, line, texture, and size to achieve design objectives
  - **Subtle:** Using variations of the same color, in sizes, shapes and textures
  - **Extreme:** Using completely different sizes, shapes, textures and color

Variety
- Differences within a piece which makes it interesting

PROPORTION

Relationship of the parts in a design to the whole
Similar to scale

Informal
- Determined by judgment and situation
- By "eye"

Formal
- Both sides of an imaginary line are the same

Golden ratio

- Proportion system in which a single line is divided into two unequal lengths to create a relationship between the smaller and larger parts

Golden section

- Golden ratio applied to a rectangle
- Found in natural and human made structures

Plants

HARDINESS

Hardiness of plants is a term used to describe their ability to survive adverse growing conditions. A plant's ability to tolerate cold, heat, drought, or wind is typically considered measurements of hardiness. In temperate latitudes, the term is most often used to describe resistance to cold, or cold-hardiness and generally measured by the lowest temperatures that a plant can withstand.

PLANT STRESS

Plant stress usually results in poor plant growth conditions.

Classification of problems

- Biotic (living organisms such as insects, fungi, slugs, and deer)
- Abiotic (non-living factors such as weather, fertility, irrigation)

Signs and symptoms

- Underdevelopment of tissues or organs
  - Examples: Stunting of plants, inadequate development of roots, malformation of leaves, inadequate production of chlorophyll and other pigments, and failure of fruits and flowers to develop.
- Overdevelopment of tissues or organs.
  - Examples: Galls on roots, stems, or leaves, witches' brooms, and profuse flowering
- Death of plant parts.
  - Examples: Wilts or diebacks, shoot or leaf blights, leaf spots, and fruit rots
- Alteration of normal appearance
  - Examples: Patterns of light and dark green on leaves, discoloration in leaves and flowers, spots

Causes

- Weather conditions
  - Too hot, too wet, too cold, too dry or some combination
  - Summer drought followed by extreme winter cold and/or a cold, wet spring followed by extreme heat.
- Human factors
  - Digging, transplanting, pruning, etc
- Poor soil composition, fertility or drainage
- Overexposure to sun

- Too shady
- Competition of weeds or even other desired plants
- Insects
  - Chewing insects (beetles, caterpillars)
  - Sucking insects (aphids, mealybugs)
  - Boring insects (bark beetles)
- Plant protection chemicals or excess/inappropriate use of any product
- Pollution of soil, air or water
- Global environmental or climate changes
  - Examples: differences in rainfall amounts, change of season length, insect or disease survival, composition of local eco-system (i.e. invasive, non-native plants) or changes in average temperatures.

PROBLEMS

Chlorosis
- Yellowing of plant leaves caused by **iron deficiency** that affects many desirable landscape plants.
  - The primary symptom of iron deficiency is the development of a yellow leaf with a network of dark green veins. In severe cases, the entire leaf turns yellow or white and the outer edges may scorch and turn brown as the plant cells die. It is common for an individual branch or one half of a tree to be chlorotic while the remainder of the tree appears normal.
- Causes of chlorosis
  - Poor drainage
  - Damaged roots
  - Compacted roots
  - High alkalinity
    - Nutrient deficiencies may occur because there is an insufficient amount in the soil or because the nutrients are unavailable due to a high pH (alkaline soil). Or the nutrients may not be absorbed due to injured roots or poor root growth.
- Treatment
  - Spraying a solution iron chelate on the leaves in the early season often provides a rapid improvement in the plant color.
  - Iron can also be injected into the tree trunk for a longer-lasting effect.
  - Soil applications of iron generally are not effective since the higher pH quickly renders this iron unavailable to the plant.

Fasciation
- An abnormality in a plant, in which a stem enlarges into a flat, ribbonlike shape resembling several stems fused together.
- Miscellaneous causes
  - Herbicides
  - Insects
  - Physical injury to the growing tip is reported to stimulate the occurrence of fasciations.
- May occur spontaneously. (inherited fasciation)
  - Example: Cockscomb celosia (Celosia argentea var. cristata) is an

Herbicide damage
- Affected leaves become distorted, twisted, curled, or cupped, and margins may turn brown.
- May kill by this treatment, but more often are stunted for a year.

Salt toxicity
- Results in varying degrees of browning of the leaf edges, especially during drought periods.
- Gradual dieback or death may occur in some salt damaged plants.

Leaf Spots
- Usually considered to be only a cosmetic problem
- round blemishes found on the leaves of many species of plants
- Mostly caused by parasitic fungi or bacteria.
- Becomes a blight or a blotch when lots of spots grow together

Powdery mildews
- Characterized by spots/patches of white to grayish, talcum powder-like growth.
- Most commonly observed on the upper side of the leaves but also affects the bottom sides of leaves, young stems, buds, flowers and young fruit.
- Infected leaves may become distorted, turn yellow with small patches of green, and fall prematurely. Infected buds may fail to open
- Requires lots of moisture to grow

SOIL pH

Measure of the acidity (sourness) or alkalinity (sweetness) of a soil. A simple numerical scale is used to express pH. The scale goes from 0.0 - 14.0, with 0.0 being most acid, and 14.0 being most alkaline. The value, 7.0 is neutral--i.e., neither acid nor alkaline.

Values
- **Acid Soil**
  - A soil with a pH<6.5
- **Alkaline Soil**
  - A soil with pH >7.3
- **Neutral Soil**
  - A soil with pH values 6.5-7.3.

Importance of pH
- For most plants, the optimum pH range is from 5.5 to 7.0
- Not an indication of fertility, but it does affect the availability of fertilizer nutrients.
- Plant nutrients are generally most available to plants in the pH range 5.5 to 6.5.

How to correct pH

- A pH determination (soil test) will tell a soil will produce good plant growth or whether it will need to be treated to adjust the pH level.
- Normally, lime or dolomite is used to increase the pH, or "sweeten" the soil.
    - Lime contains mainly calcium carbonate
    - Dolomite contains both calcium carbonate and magnesium carbonate.

Note: The greater the amount of organic matter or clay in a soil, the more lime or dolomite required to change the pH.

LAWNS AND GRASSES

Chemical weed control is not recommended on newly planted grasses until at least 2 months after establishment.

Types of turf grasses
- **Warm season grasses**
    - Actively grow from mid-April to mid-October
    - Produce plants and help grasses fill in areas and recuperate after being stressed
- **Cool season grasses**
    - Grow best during the spring and fall seasons when it is cool
    - Grow in bunches
    - Need uniform seed distribution when seeding cool season grasses to avoid bunchy turf

Planting time
- **North**
    - Spring or fall, when soil is naturally moist, and day temperatures reach 55ºF. / 40ºF night.
    - Most rapid growth occurs spring, fall.
- **South**
    - Plant in mid to late spring, when day temperatures reach 70ºF. / 50ºF night
    - Most rapid growth occurs later spring to late summer

Planting Methods
- **Seeded**
- **Vegetative planting with sprigs, plugs, and solid sod**
    - **Sod**
        - A mat of living grass plants consisting of blades, roots and soil which has been severed from its growing bed in such a manner as to permit transplanting in its entirety
    - **Plugs**
        - Approximately 2" square
    - **Sprigs**
        - Shredded sod

Pesticide
A substance intended to prevent, kill or repel pests.
- Common classes of pesticides include insecticides, herbicides, fungicides, rodenticides, disinfectants, and wood preservatives

Erosion control methods

- Revegetation: introducing grasses, flowers, ground covers and even shrubs and trees to a erosion vulnerable area
- Different mulches
- Erosion control products known as tackifiers, or binders
- Netting blankets
- Porous matting

Soil

- Have a soil test run before the soil is prepared so that fertilizer deficiencies may be corrected as well as pH.
- After the soil test results have been returned, work any recommended materials into the upper 6" of soil.

Soil for containers

- Use a well-drained, light-weight potting mix designed for growing containerized plants.
- Select containers with drain holes as excellent drainage is essential

Tree protection

- Tree grates and tree protectors are often used to protect the tree and provide safety to pedestrian

Edging

- Border plants
- Mowing strips
- Manufactured edgings of plastic and metal
- Natural edgings such as stones

Grass pavers

- Hollow pavers used for the construction of permeable pavements.

INTERIOR PLANTS

Light

- **Low:** Minimum light level of 25' candles, preferred level of 75' to 200' candles.
  - Areas more than eight feet from windows as in the center of a room, a hallway or an inside wall
- **Medium:** Minimum of 71' to 100' candles, preferred level of 200' to 500' candles
  - Locations in a range of 4' – 8' from south and east windows and west windows that do not receive direct sun.
- **High:** Minimum of 200' candles, preferred level of 500' to 1000' candles.
  - Within 4' of large south-east or west facing windows
- **Very high:** Minimum of 1000'candles, preferred level of1000' candles.

Moisture

- **Dry:** Does not need very much water and can stand low humidity.
- **Moist:** Requires a moderate amount of water and loves some humidity in the atmosphere.
- **Wet:** Usually requires more water than other plants and must have high humidity in its surroundings.

Soil

All potting soils include two or more ingredients such as peat to hold water, perlite to give aeration, and bark or vermiculite to hold nutrients. These should be thoroughly and uniformly mixed for good root growth

- **Heavy Mix:** Does not drain
- **Medium mix:** Adequate drainage
- **Light Mix:** Drains readily

Plant food

- **General rate:** One teaspoon soluble house plant fertilizer per gallon of water or follow recommendations on package.
- **Low:** No application in winter during dormant periods.
- **Medium:** Apply every other month during winter and every month during spring and summer.
- **High:** Apply every month during winter and twice each month during the spring and summer.

Temperature

The desirable temperatures for humans fall within the optimum range for most foliage and flowering plants.

- Daytime temperatures of 70º–80º
- Nighttime range of 60º–70º

Containers

As a rule, the diameter of the pot should be about one-third the height of the plant from the top of the foliage to the soil line

- Plants with shallow roots (like cacti) grow best in shallow containers.
- Deep-rooted plants need more room to grow and require a taller container.

LANDSCAPING FOR SLOPES

Slopes

- **Easy slope:**
  - Slopes less than 1' vertical to 4' horizontal (25%)
  - Require no special landscape treatment and solutions for circulation
  - Riding and gang mowers may be used safely and efficiently
- **Moderate Slope**
  - Slopes from 1' vertical to 4' horizontal (25%) to 1' vertical on 3' horizontal (33%)
  - Hand movers are manageable.
  - Plant grass where accessible
  - Avoid single specimens of trees and shrubs on these grades in grass due to the problems of mowing around them - use only in groups or bed plantings.

- **Steep Slope**:
  - Slopes from 1' vertical to 3' horizontal (33%) to 1' vertical on 2' horizontal (50%)
  - Hand movers are not easily manageable.
  - Creates water drainage problem
  - Requires the building of terraces or steps across the slope to divert water away from slopes and prevent soil erosion.
  - If the slope is gentle, seeding grass may be enough.
- **Severe Slope**
  - Slopes 1' vertical to 2' horizontal (50%) and steeper
  - Difficult to establish vegetation and plants, to maintain and to prevent erosion

Guidelines for landscaping slopes

- Always contact local building department before embarking on any landscape construction project
- Leave larger earth moving jobs to a professional
- Consider installing terraced gardens on slopes to allow heavy rains to soak in rather than to runoff and cause erosion.
- Place lower-water demand plants at the tops of slopes and higher-demand plants at the bottom.
- Consider using groundcovers with lower water requirements for slopes and hard-to-mow locations.
- Avoid using turf in areas less than 10' wide and on slopes steeper than 4:1. Although turf provides effective erosion-control, maintaining regularly mowed turf on a steep slope can be difficult and dangerous.
- Consider where plant shadows will be

TREE PLANTING

Proper Planting

- Plant at the depth where the roots spread from the trunk usually the same depth as it stood in the nursery bed.
- Do expose the trunk flare (stem tissue) at the base of the trunk.
- Make a dish. (shallow and wide)
- Loosen the soil far beyond the dripline of the tree
- Check for tightly compressed or 'potbound' roots.
- Carefully loosen the fine roots away from the tight mass and then spread the roots prior to planting.
- Brace the tree only if it will not remain upright in a moderate wind
- Brace with broad, belt-like materials that won't injure the bark (CAMB GUARDS).
- Mulch with composted material approximately 3-4" thick.
- Keep mulch at least 6" (15cm.) away from the trunk to reduce chances of rodent injury and infection by pathogens
- Keep soil moist, not water-logged, to the depth of the roots.
- Water out to drip line so the roots will grow outward.
- Remove dead and dying branches properly.
- Wait until the second growing season after planting to begin training cuts for shaping and to begin fertilization with organic material if needed.

Planting Balled and Burlapped Trees
- Cut away completely (mandatory, in the case of synthetic or plastic burlap) or at least pulled back from the top third of the ball (in the case of natural burlap)
- Removed any string or twine

Planting Container Trees
- Remove the container completely (metal or plastic)
- Tear the sides away (fiber containers)

Planting Bare-Rooted Trees
- Inspect the roots to ensure that they are moist and have numerous lengths of fine root hairs (healthy).
- Plant as soon as possible.
- Keep moist in the period between purchase and planting.
- Prune broken or damaged roots but save as much as possible
- Build a cone of earth in the center of the hole around which to splay the roots.
- Make sure that when properly seated on this cone the tree is planted so that the 'trunk flare' is clearly visible and the 'crown', where the roots and top meet, is about 2" above the soil level.

FALL PLANTING

Fall happens to be one of the better times for planting many kinds of plants. The earlier plants are started the better the plants survival will be. In general, a planting window from mid to late August to mid-October can be safely used for fall planting in zones 4 and 5. In warmer zones this window may be a bit longer. The top of the plant may not continue to grow in the fall season, but the root system of a plant does.

If planted early enough a plant established in the fall of the year has a better chance of survival during the sometimes stressful summer months when air temperatures are higher and rain isn't as plentiful. Because it has grown a bit (at the roots) in the fall, it is ready to start growing as early as it can when spring arrives. In the fall, air temperatures, soil temperatures and moisture levels are generally more moderate and stable that promotion of rapid root development is enhanced.

PLANT SELECTION

Primary elements of design
Primary elements of design are the first elements looked at when determining plant materials.
- Plant type (e.g., tree, shrub, vine and groundcover)
- Height and width
- Texture
- Form
- Seasonal interest or color

Secondary Elements of Design:
Secondary elements are used when narrowing down the types of plants used.
- Drought tolerance
- Insect and disease resistance
- Environmental tolerance (wind, pollution, cold)
- Soil adaptability
- Full sun or shade tolerance
- Moisture tolerance

Selecting Plants in the Nursery
The quality of the trees, shrubs, vines, and ground covers selected in a nursery can be just as important as species selection, site evaluation, planting, and maintenance in determining their success in the landscape. Carefully inspect plants from top to bottom before purchase to ensure that they are healthy, vigorous, and free from injury, disease, and pests.

MULCH

Any material such as leaves, bark, straw or other materials left loose and applied to the soil surface for the beneficial purpose of reducing evaporation. Bulk quantities of mulch are sold in cubic yard volumes.

Benefits of Mulch
- Helps prevent the germination of many weed seeds, reducing the need for cultivation or the use of herbicides
- Help moderate the soil temperature (Three inches of mulch keeps the root zone of a plant cool and moist even in hot weather)
- Retains moisture during dry weather, reducing the need for watering
- Protects roots from frost in cold weather
- Builds good organic soil structure
- Protects the soil from the impact of raindrops that can cause crusting

Types of mulch
- **Organic mulches**
  - May break down in one season or less or persist for more than one season
  - Used mainly in vegetable and flower gardens or around newly planted trees and shrubs
  - Usually decomposed enough by the end of the growing season that they can be spaded or plowed under, increasing the organic matter content of the soil and thereby improving soil structure
    - Examples: Bark, pine needles, wood chips
- **Inorganic mulches**
  - Not as beneficial to plants as the organic mulches are because they do not improve the structure or nutrient content of the soil.
    - Examples: Spun-bonded or woven landscape fabrics (geo-textiles)
  - Black plastic mulch is not recommended for use in the landscape but may be useful in the vegetable garden.

  Note: Though not generally considered mulches, some low-growing ground cover plants produce many of the same benefits as mulch. They shade the soil surface, keeping it cool in summer and at the same time preventing evaporation.

How to mulch

- Check with your local agricultural extension or garden center for advice on the best mulch to use in your area
- Apply the mulch upon planting or in late spring after your region's last frost date. (Needs adequately warmed soil for good plant growth)
- Spread the mulch 1 to 6" thick, depending on the size and sturdiness of the plant.
- Maintain a 4" to 6" mulch-free area adjacent to the woody stems to reduce damage from rot, insects and voles

How Much Mulch

To calculate the amount of mulch needed:

- Measure the area to be mulched, in square feet. (100 square feet)
- Convert the desired depth (3") to a fraction of a foot.
  - Example: 3" divided by 12" equals ¼ ' or 0.25'.
- Multiply this fraction by the square foot measurement of the area to be covered (.25' x 100 square feet = 25 cubic feet).
- Convert cubic feet to cubic yards by dividing cubic feet by 27 (25/27 = .926).

STAKING/GUYING A TREE

- Problems:
  - The root ball of a newly planted but unstaked tree will tend to roll or pivot in the ground, resulting in tree lean or blow-over
  - Trunk movement from strong wind, at or below the soil line, will break the root ball, destroying roots and resulting in a wobbly tree.
- Most deciduous trees 5' to 6' or larger are candidates for staking when planted on an exposed site.
- The larger the tree, the more important it is to provide extra support. Usually, a deciduous tree up to 1½ to 1¾ inches in caliper (10 to 12' in height) can be staked.
- Stakes should be removed after one growing season, but may remain in place for a second season only if additional support is required.

Note: Current research seems to suggest that such practices may be more harmful than good.

PLANTING SCHEME (SCHENME PLANTING)

- Combination of plants (may be single or area plantings), surrounded by a shape
- Can be applied singularly, linear or as an area whereby the arrangement is either schematic (similar to area planting) or detailed.
- Usually used for plantings in the free 'open' landscape but can also be detailed e.g. hedges, borders.
  - Example: Informal English cottage garden, Coastal planting

INTERIOR LANDSCAPING

Interior landscaping is also known as plantscaping and interiorscaping.
A landscaped area or areas within the shortest circumferential line defining the perimeter or exterior boundary of the parking or loading area, or similar paved area, excluding driveways or walkways providing access to the facility (as applied to parking and loading facilities or to similar paved areas).

URBAN LANDSCAPING

An urban soil is one that has been disturbed or contaminated through urban development, and no longer has characteristics like the natural landscape surrounding the developed area.

Characteristics of urban soils
- High degree of variability in soil horizons.
- Lack of topsoil due to removal or burial by developers
- Compaction
- Restricted water movement, aeration and water drainage due to compaction
- Surface crust
- Higher pH of subsoil
- Greater soil temperature fluctuations
- Excessively high soil temperatures due to masses of concrete and paving
- Lack of the natural cycles of nutrient recycling is usually no longer present in urban landscapes due to removal of vegetation growth.

Soil Problems
- Buried debris
- Soil contaminants
- Inappropriate soil chemistry
- Settlement
- Stressful environmental condition

LOW MAINTAINENCE LANDSCAPE

There is no such thing as a landscape that takes care of itself. Proper planning, selection, and installation of landscape plants and structures will reduce the amount of time a landscape requires to look its best. Advance planning can result in an attractive and functional landscape that reduces the long-term maintenance cost of any landscape project. Factors to consider include the following:
- **Size**
  - Reducing size is often the most straightforward and successful way to reduce landscape maintenance.
- **Simplicity**
  - Eliminate as many frills such as bird baths, statues, and flower beds as possible
- **Arrangement**
  - Scattered, cluttered plant groups need hand edging and weeding and complicate your mowing.

- **Grass/Ground cover**
  - Avoid planting grass in areas that are too shady, too dry or wet, or too steep to be mowed safely.
- **Mulches**
  - Use mulches around plants to minimize weeds and conserve moisture.
- **Fertilizer**
  - Plants kept at minimum fertilization levels need less pruning or mowing than highly-fertilized plants.
- **Tree beds**
  - A gravel bed or ground cover around trees eliminates trimming and speeds mowing
- **Edging**
  - Metal or brick edging between the lawn and gravel walks or drives and around tree beds eliminates tedious trimming, keeps stones out of the lawn, and keeps grass from growing into walks and driveways.
- **Paths**
  - Make sure all access walks, paths, and gates are wide enough for lawn-maintenance equipment and pave areas with concrete or spread compacted crushed stone or gravel.
- **Pruning**
  - Prune trees so the wind can through them without causing damage.
- **Native plants**
  - Use native plants that are already adapted to local climate extremes (heat, cold, drought, or available sunlight) and soil characteristics (type and drainage) and to pest problems.
- **Low maintenance plants**
  - Select plants that do not require excessive maintenance such as spraying and pruning.
- **Quality plants**
  - Shop at reputable nurseries and garden. Select plants for USDA hardiness zones
- **Quality grades**
  - Select plants tagged according to the grades and standards set by plant industry. Choose a No. 1 plant if possible.
- **Good planting practices**
  - Select the proper planting site and to prepare the hole for planting.
- **Preventative maintenance**
  - Anticipate problems before they occur. A preventive maintenance program decreases maintenance time.

Shading

Shade is a much-appreciated commodity. When designing for shade it is important to become familiar with the shade pattern in a landscape. This pattern is influenced by the sun's path and by plantings and structures in surrounding area as well as adjacent areas.

SHADE PATTERN

- **Deep or full**
  - No direct sunlight
    - Example: Under the canopy of a dense tree, a roof, or an overhang

- **Open shade**
  - Open to the sky but do not receive any direct sun.
    - Example: location shaded by a tall building or wall.
- **Partial shade**
  - Receives five hours or less of direct sunshine during the day
    - Examples: east-facing wall receives morning sun only
- **Filtered or dappled shade**
  - Found under open-branched trees or lathes
  - May be relatively bright, without receiving any direct sun

CREATING SHADE

- Strategically placed trees and shrubs
- An overhead arbor
- Vine-covered trellis
- Decorative walls or fences of varying heights
- Place seating area to take advantage of shaded areas

Playground Design

PLAYGROUND EQUIPMENT AND STRUCTURES

Composite Play Structures
- According to ASTM F 1487, this means "two or more play structures, attached or functionally linked," creating one integral unit with more than one play activity.

Critical Height: Standard measure of shock attenuation
- According to CPSC No. 325, this means "the fall height below which a life-threatening head injury would not be expected to occur."

Fall Height
- According to ASTM F 1487, this means "the vertical distance between a designated play surface and the protective surfacing beneath it." The fall height of playground equipment should not exceed the Critical Height of the protective surfacing beneath it.

Play Structure
- According to ASTM F 1487, this is "a free-standing structure with one or more components and their supporting members."

Protective Surfacing
- According to ASTM F 1487, this means impact-attenuating "materials to be used within the use zone of any playground equipment" for playground surface systems

Transfer Point
- According to ASTM F 1487, this is "a platform or deck along an accessible route of travel or an accessible platform provided to allow a child in a wheelchair to transfer from the chair onto the equipment."

Use Zone
- According to ASTM F 1487, this is "the area beneath and immediately adjacent to a play structure that is designated for unrestricted circulation around the equipment and on whose surface it is predicted that a user would land when falling from or exiting the equipment."

PLAYGROUND SURFACE SYSTEMS

Safety Surfacing Standards
- ASTM F1292 Standard Specification for Impact Attenuation for Surface Systems Under and Around Playground Equipment.
- ASTM F1951 (formerly PS83) Standard Specification for Determination of Accessibility of Surface Systems Under and Around Playground Equipment.
- ASTM F 2075 Standard Specification for Engineered Wood Fiber for Use as a Playground Safety Surface Under and Around Playground Equipment.

Types of surfacing
- Loose-fill
  - Examples are shredded wood products, sand, gravel, and shredded rubber
- Unitary
  - Examples are rubber mats with a poured-in-place top surface and synthetic poured surfaces.

BENCH DESIGN

Size — Fixed and have seats that are 20" (510 mm) minimum to 24" (610 mm) maximum in depth and 42" (1065 mm) minimum in length

Back Support — Back support that is 42" (1065 mm) minimum in length and extends from a point 2" (51 mm) maximum above the seat to a point 18" (455 mm) minimum above the seat

Seat Height — From 17" (430 mm) minimum to 19" (485 mm) maximum above the floor or ground

Structural Strength — Allowable stresses not to exceed for materials used when a vertical or horizontal force of 250 lbs. (1112 N) is applied at any point on the seat, fastener, mounting device, or supporting structure.

Wet Locations — The surface of benches installed in wet locations shall be slip-resistant and shall not accumulate water.

Site Design

REQUIREMENTS

Landscape architects are expected to

- Develop site or land use plans that take into consideration the off-site an on-site influences to development.
- Consider various codes, consultant studies and principles of sustainability when creating a site design.
- Evaluate the design solutions of others
- Create alternative solutions to a problem.
- Develop design, planning, and management solutions considering on-site and off-site influences
- Convey the information through text and in drawings.
- Incorporate consultant studies into your design
- Predict the implications of your design, planning, and management proposals on the natural and cultural systems both within the site and in the larger context.
- Evaluate design alternatives to determine the appropriate solution
- Create design alternatives to demonstrate the range of options.
- Incorporate into design solutions. circulation systems such as
  - Equestrian
  - Bicycle
  - Pedestrian
  - Vehicular systems

PROBLEM TYPES

- Site, circulation, access and parking
- Site land use
- Detailed site design
- Planting layout and lighting design for a site
- Hardscape and planting design
- Conceptual site design
- Written analysis of problem criteria

PROCEDURE

- Review problem criteria as it often gives options which direct how to proceed.(problem statement, context, required sections)
- Carefully note any detail as well as implicit instructions.
- Identify all required design criteria in the LARE reference Manual that will determine the available **area** for the design solutions (setbacks, easements)

- Refer to LARE *Reference Manual* for the graphic conventions and requirements for problem criteria that will direct the **layout** of the design solution
  - Parking, areas, service turnarounds and drive-through areas
  - Approved list of lighting
  - Approved list plant materials

- o Pedestrian Security/Safety (clear zone requirements)
- o Guardrails and barriers
- o Accessible route, ramps, stairs and handrails
- Address views

- Choose locations for design criteria such as
  - o Site building
  - o Access Points
  - o Circulation
  - o Driveways
  - o Parking
  - o Drop-offs
  - o Turnarounds
  - o Loading dock
  - o Lawn area
  - o Privacy area
  - o Play area
  - o Benches
  - o Tables
  - o Walkways
  - o Trails
  - o Buffering of building and high-intensity use areas

- Prepare a planting plan that may
  - o Accent
  - o Screen
  - o Create privacy
  - o Create focal area
  - o Be formal or informal

- Draw a **lighting plan** that provides a
  - o Hierarchy of fixtures:
    - Tall downlights
    - Low downlights
    - Bollards and uplights as accents
  - o Footcandle (lux) distribution patterns

- Address code for handicap accessibility
  - o Should be near and entry
  - o Minimum design criteria for turning radii

- Include all necessary graphic conventions, labels, notes and other types of information to complete the design.

TIPS

- Always check the LARE *Reference Manual* for applicable codes and requirements.
- Pay attention to all details.
- Stick with simple solutions.
- Provide additional labels that demonstrate an understanding of the detailed design criteria for all aspects of the solution
- Use correct grammar, spelling and sentence structure to communicate any written response
- Avoid using bullets in written response

Section 4: Grading, Drainage, and Construction Documentation

Water Management

REQUIREMENTS

Landscape architects will be tested on their ability to
- Manipulate landforms to convey runoff, meet design requirements, and minimize environmental impact.
- Evaluate the impact of their decisions on existing off-site conditions
- Develop strategies for water conservation and preservation of land resources.
- Develop grading and drainage plans considering on-site and off-site influences and convey the information in drawings.
- Manipulate contours to demonstrate your ability to convey water to meet design requirements while protecting land and water resources.
- Evaluate existing landforms and drainage systems to locate program elements minimizing environmental or economic impacts.
- Think 3-dimensionally to manipulate land forms to meet design requirements

PROBLEM TYPES

Develop grading and drainage plans
- For the plane surface of a slope or terraced site
- For the surface of an at-grade site
- For a road, curb and sidewalk to drain runoff
- For a site (Sloped) for a building
- To site a building in an environmentally sensitive area (watershed)
- By using "plan and profile" to establish the grades on a surface
- By using the rational method formula to establish the grades on a surface
- By using a viewing cone to screen an objectionable element from a viewing area
- To site a building on a hilltop or knoll
- With surface and subsurface drainage
- Analyze drainage

PROCEDURE

- Review problem criteria as it often gives **options** which direct how to proceed.(problem statement, context, required sections)
- Carefully note any detail and/or implicit instructions.
  - Example:
    - All runoff must be intercepted and disposed of
    - Existing catch basins and existing swales reveal a part of the solution that pertains to drainage
    - Existing contours help to understand runoff flow patterns
- Identify all required design criteria in the LARE reference Manual that will determine the available area for the design solutions (setbacks, easements)
- Refer to LARE *Reference Manual* for the graphic conventions and requirements for problem criteria that will direct the layout of the design solution
- Determine the finish surface (FS) elevation
  - Determine the required spot elevations using the difference in elevation formula
  - Calculate the grade using the grade formula
- Determine and plot the whole number contour line using the length formula
- Determine the cross slope (short axis) using the cross-slope formula to calculate the deflection
- Plot and number the whole-number contour lines.

- Determine the flowline for drainage.
  - May require a swale
  - Usually does not need to continue beyond the lowest end of the element being protected
  - May have variable grade (contours may not need to be evenly spaced)
  - Calculate the high-point elevation
  - Determine where the first whole number contour should cross the flow line
  - Determine the points where the remaining whole number contours cross the flow line
  - Grade the backslope and frontslope so contours meet required slope ratio.

- Complete required design criteria which includes the following:
  - Add remaining existing contours
  - Add tick marks at points where revised contours meet existing one
  - Number all existing and revised contour lines
  - Add flow arrows and grade callouts

TIPS

- Pay close attention to any details to avoid violating health, safety or welfare issues
- Note the scale of the drawing
- Note the orientation of north. It may not always be up
- Note the contour interval as it is not always 1".
- Offsets or breaks in the contour lines indicate that a finished surface
- Determine a minimum workable elevation
- Try to anticipate all of the whole-number contour lines that will be required to complete the plot.
- Study the topography
  - High, low, flat, sloping

- o Steep or shallow grade
- o Drainage features (Watercourse, manmade drainage devices)
- o Direction of runoff (If it flows toward a structure it will most likely be diverted with a horseshoe swale)
- Note the location of drainage structures as it usually reveal part of the solution
- Runoffs should not be permitted to run onto the design site
- Run-off naturally flows from a high point to a low point
- Avoid creating an inverted curb, one that is below the road surface rather than 6" above.
- When required to delineate a ridgeline, complete it first before siting the rest of the problem criteria.
- When required to use the rational formula it is better to solve that portion of the problem first in order to meet slope problem criteria during the site grading phase of the solution
- When required to screen an problem element from viewing mounding must be used.(Determine the minimum workable elevation by drawing a simple section)
- When required to show contour lines as offset at the edge of a finished surface, indicate it as a flat-topped ridgeline with the contour lines pointing downward.
- Try to visually what the finished design should look like.

Ecosystems

The living and nonliving things that interact in an environment make up an ecosystem. An ecosystem is made up of smaller parts that include populations, communities, and habitats, as well as nonliving things, such as air, sunlight, and soil. Nature and living things can change ecosystems. Sometimes, the ecosystem can be changed so much that the plants and animals can no longer live there. Whenever people move into an area, the ecosystem is changed. Changes that can harm the environment include removing trees (causes soil erosion), destroying habitats (causes animals to leave and plants die), and polluting the water and air (causes harm to plants and animals). Some human activities can even destroy ecosystems. Water surfaces, mountains, caves, and the arctic are examples of ecosystems.

- Freshwater ecosystems - lakes, rivers, ponds, streams, and some marshes
- Saltwater ecosystems - oceans, seas, marshes, and a few lakes
- Forest ecosystems Deciduous, Coastal, Coniferous

TYPES OF ECOSYSTEMS

Bog (Peat Bog) — An area having a wet, spongy, acidic substrate (soil) composed chiefly of sphagnum moss and peat in which characteristic shrubs and herbs and sometimes trees grow. Bogs have organic soil, unlike other wetlands, which have mineral soils

Boreal forest — A forest made up mostly of conifers, such as that reaching across North America from Newfoundland to Alaska.

Fen — Low marshy ground containing peat that is rich in mineral salts and is alkaline rather than acidic

Grassland — A natural community where the dominant plants are grasses

Meadows — A term used to describe a field of permanent grass used for hay, but also applied to rich, waterside grazing areas that are not suitable for arable cultivation.

Marsh — An area of soft, wet, low-lying land, characterized by grassy vegetation that is not woody and often forms a transition zone between water and land

Playa — A shallow central basin of a plain where water gathers after a rain and is evaporated

Riparian wetland — A narrow zone of habitats, which may or may not be vegetated, directly associated with streamsides or lake shores, or similar immediately adjacent habitat

Salt marsh — Areas of brackish, shallow water usually found in coastal areas and in deltas Also inland marshes in arid areas where the water has a high salt level because of evaporation

Swamp — A forested or shrub-scrub wetland, contrasting with a marsh that has non-woody plants

ECOLOGICAL SITE PLANNING CHARACTERISTICS

Disturb the site as little as possible by doing the following.
- Minimize storm water runoff
- Minimize habitat disturbance
- Avoid sensitive areas such as wetlands and regionally important ecosystems (tidal saltwater marshes, oak-hickory savanna, grass prairies, boreal forest)
- Buffer and accentuate areas of importance on a site
- Protect open space
- Reduce the risk of erosion
- Save energy by providing for passive solar, natural ventilation, and day lighting

ECOLOGICAL SITE DESCRIPTION

The data comprising an ecological site description is presented in four major categories:

Site Characteristics — Identifies the site and describes the physiographic, climate, soil, and water features associated with the site.

Plant Communities — Describes the ecological dynamics and the common plant communities comprising the various vegetation states of the site

Site Interpretations — Interpretive information pertinent to the use and management of the site and its related resources

Supporting Information — Provides information on sources of information and data utilized in developing the site description and the relationship of the site to other

CONCEPTS

Biomass — Any organic matter which is available on a renewable basis through natural processes, like forests, grasslands, crop lands, or salt marshes

Ecology — Study of the interactions of living organisms with one another and with their nonliving environment of matter and energy; study of the structure and function of nature

Fauna — A list of the animals living in a particular ecosystem

Flora — The species of plants found in a particular area (in contrast to "fauna", the animals of a particular area; note that even colorful flower-like butterflies are fauna, and not flora!). Also, a book listing and usually describing the species of plants found in a particular area.

Mangrove — Plant communities and trees that inhabit tidal swamps, muddy silt, and sand banks at the mouths of rivers and other low-lying areas which are regularly inundated by the sea, but which are protected from strong waves and currents. Mangroves are the only woody species that will grow where the land is periodically flooded with sea water

Meadow — Typically, a level grassland or field within a larger ecosystem, such as a forest Often, the grass grown on its natural, low-lying, moist areas is used for forage or fodder or cut for hay

PRESERVATION/REHABILITATION

Farmland preservation plan
- Protecting and preserving large contiguous blocks of agricultural land while enabling farmers to operate their businesses at a profit
- May voluntarily enroll in programs and receive special benefits and protection

Façade and Landscapes Rehabilitation Grant
Eligible projects may receive grant awards to rehabilitate facades and landscape
Factors considered include:
- Architectural integrity and physical condition
- Structural system
- Material damage
- Material quality
- Design quality
- Presence of ornamentation

Criteria for obtaining a neighborhood building and landscape rehabilitation assistance grant
- Renovation and restoration
- Encourage good design projects and workmanship
- Preserve unique historic character
- Promote beautification and use of open space

Historic area
- An area or building in which historic events occurred, or one which has special value due to architectural or cultural features relating to the heritage of the community.

Rehabilitation
- Process of returning a property to a state of utility, through repair or alteration, which makes possible an efficient contemporary use while preserving those portions and features of the property which are significant to its historic, architectural, and cultural values

Rehabilitation grant program
- The word "grant" refers to a sum of money given to support the work of an agency, organization, or (occasionally) individual, usually as a result of a formal decision-making process involving a written or oral presentation and review. Grants are distinct from loans in that they are given outright, with no conditions for repayment.

Examples:
- Development and preservation of residential areas within a physical environment that is healthy, safe, convenient and attractive
- Preservation, development and redevelopment of a variety of suitable industrial and commercial sites in terms of both physical characteristics and location

Rehabilitated landscape
- Any relandscaping project that requires a permit

Wetland preservation plan
- Designed to protect, sustain, and restore wetland systems

Low Impact Design

Low impact design (LID) is an approach to environmentally friendly land use planning with emphasis on hydrologic functions.
- Reduce the volume of runoff
- Decentralize flows

PRACTICES

LID techniques capture water on site, filter it through vegetation, and let it soak into the ground where it can recharge the local water table rather than being lost as surface runoff. This is usually accomplished by creating a series of smaller retention/detention areas that allow localized filtration rather than carrying runoff to a remote collection area.

Common strategies include

- **Bio-retention cells**
  - o Typically consist of grass buffers, sand beds, a ponding area for excess runoff storage, organic layers, planting soil and vegetation
  - o Provides storage area, away from buildings and roadways, where stormwater collects and filters into the soil.
  - o Permanent ponds May incorporated permanent ponds as landscaping features
  - o Have also been called rain gardens since they are typically landscaped wit native plants and grasses, selected according to their moisture requirements and ability to tolerate pollutants
  - o Requires annual maintenance to replace mulching materials, remove accumulated silt, or revitalize soils
- **Swale**
  - o Shallow open earth channel used to intercept and route surface water flows to a discharge location
  - o An alternative to curb and gutter systems
  - o Usually along residential streets or highways
  - o Use grasses or other vegetation to reduce runoff velocity and allow filtration
- **Filter strips**
  - o Can be designed as landscape features within parking lots or other areas, to collect flow from large impervious surfaces
  - o May direct water into vegetated detention areas or special sand filters that capture pollutants and gradually discharge water over a period of time
- **Disconnected impervious areas**
  - o Direct water flows collected from structures, driveways, or street sections, into separate localized detention cells instead of combining it in drainpipes with other runoff.
  - o Limits the velocity and overall amount of conveyed water that must be handled by end-of-pipe facilities

- **Cistern collection systems**
  - o Can be designed to store rainwater for dry-period irrigation, rather than channeling it to streams
    - ▪ Examples: Rain barrels

Conservation of Natural Resources

STOCKPILING NATIVE TOPSOIL

Native topsoil is an important natural resource that contains a diverse fungal community that is essential for plant health. Stockpiled onsite for use after projects are completed.

If space and funds allow, the task of establishing plantings can be avoided by keeping the plant and soil structure intact using a front-end loader to remove topsoil in sections. The sections can then be stored for the duration of the project.

Methods to maintain microbial health (fungi community)
Sustainable practices should be used when storing topsoil.
- Store topsoil in several small batches as less likely to become compacted
  - 6' for sandy soils
  - 4' feet for clay soils to maintain mycorrhizal health
- Cover by a breathable material.

Note: Deep stockpiles, heavy traffic, repeated handling, and excavation when soils are extremely wet or dry compromises soil porosity and should be avoided. (Norman et. al. 1997)

Cover material for stockpiles
- Geosynthetic, such as a filtration fabric
- Fast-growing plantings
  - Preferred
  - Can be tilled under to provide additional nutrients
- Geosynthetic and fast-growing plantings

Length of storage
- Stockpiling soil for more than a month will likely kill mycorrhizae

Subsoil
- Soil underneath the topsoil which is of low quality for vegetative purposes

Top Soil
- High grade quality of dirt with an increased concentration of nutrients which is mostly used for plant growth and as a lawn base for areas high in clay or rock.
- Upper 6 to 8"of soil

Fill Dirt
- This material is used to fill in large areas which will then be covered with the top soil. Fill dirt is a lower grade dirt and is not ideal for plant or lawn growth. It is used only as a compactable base or fill.

TREE PROTECTION
- Determine the **Critical Root Zone (CRZ)** for each tree, which is roughly a circle with a radius equal to the average dripline
  - Most tree roots are in the top 2' of soil, and that feeding roots are in the top few inches.
  - Roots require non-compacted soil for both air and moisture.
- Protect at least 75% of the CRZ.
- Fence the area to prevent traffic or storage of materials. If fencing is not possible, cover the CRZ with 6" – 8" of wood chip mulch and ¾" plywood or road boards to prevent soil compaction.
- Route underground utilities to avoid CRZ.
  - If digging is unavoidable, bore under the roots or hand dig to avoid severing them.

- Design paving away from CRZ.
  - If this is not possible, use a porous material for driveways, such as crushed granite, pavestone, etc.
- Save trees that are very close to buildings by using pier-and-beam construction techniques that allow air and moisture to reach the root zone

Storm water Management

Functions associated with planning, designing, constructing, maintaining, financing, and regulating the facilities (both constructed and natural) that collect, store, control, and/or convey stormwater.

DRAINAGE

Drainage is the interception, collection and removal of excess stormwater from an area into another area or into a receiving water body. The system can be:
- **Enclosed**
  - Consisting of essentially continuous pipes and/or box culverts below the ground surface
- **Open**
  - Consisting of open channels, either natural or improved, with only comparatively short lengths enclosed by pipes or culverts

FACTORS THAT AFFECT DRAINAGE

Apron
- A floor or lining to protect a surface from erosion
  - Example: Pavement below chutes, spillways, or at the toes of dams

Berm
- A constructed barrier of compacted earth

Grading
- The cutting and/or filling of the land surface to a desired slope or elevation.

Impervious surface
- Any hard surface that does not readily permit water to infiltrate
  - Examples: Walkways, patios, driveways, parking lots

Pervious Surfaces
- Any surface that absorbs water such as undeveloped areas, fields, yards and other unpaved areas

Soil creep
- Slow, down slope movement of soil caused by thermal expansion and contraction of the surface, alternate wetting and drying of the soil

Time of Concentration
- Time at which outflow from a basin is equal to inflow or time of equilibrium.

Water table (phreatic surface, groundwater table)
- Top of the water surface in the saturated part of an aquifer
- May increase the chance of drainage problems and wetland conflicts

RUNOFF

Water originating from rainfall and other precipitation that ultimately flows into drainage facilities, rivers, and streams

Classification of factors that affect runoff
- **Permanent Factors**
  - Slope of basin, soil structure, vegetation, channel density
- **Transient Factors**
  - Associated size, intensity, and duration of rainfall

Factors that affect the rate and volume of runoff
- Rainfall
  - Duration
  - Intensity
  - Distribution
- Land Surface
  - Watershed size, shape, and orientation relative to storms
  - Topography (slope, depressional areas, etc.)
  - Geology and soils
  - Human factors (agriculture, silviculture, dams, development)
  - Water status of soil

Runoff coefficient
- A number expressed as a decimal/percentage that describes how much water will run off a site or surface
- Typical items associated with coefficient of runoff are landscape bedding, rooftops and turf grass
  - Example: Runoff coefficient of 1.0 indicates that 100% of the water will run off a soil type and land use.

SWALES

Shallow channel with at least a 3:1 side slope which is designed to force water to flow as sheet flow along its length. Usually planted with grasses and/or other dense vegetation to slow the flow of water and trap sediment and other pollutants.

Dry swale
- Designed to completely store the runoff volume and filter it through soil before it is collected by an underdrain
- Contain standing water only for a very short period

Vegetated swale

- A long, narrow trapezoidal or circular-shaped channel, planted with a variety of trees, shrubs and grasses. Stormwater runoff from impervious surfaces is directed through the swale, where water velocity is slowed and in some cases infiltrated, allowing pollutants to settle out.
- Uses check dams to create small ponded areas to facilitate infiltration treating stormwater runoff

Wet swale

- Acts much like small wetlands. Water exits the swale over a small weir.
- Can be effective at removing pollutants where the water table is very close to the surface and a dry swale is not feasible

FLOODING

Flood Hazard Areas

- Areas in an identified flood plain

Flood insurance rate map (FIRM)

- A flood map published by the Federal Insurance Administration developed from a community flood study and used to produce actuarial rates.
- Once this map is complete, a community is eligible for the National Flood Insurance Program.
- Rates developed from this map are termed pre-FIRM or post-FIRM, depending on when a building is constructed.

Flood map

- Risk assessment tool used to help determine the different flooding risks in a community.
- The most current maps, called Digital Flood Insurance Rate Maps, depict high-, medium- and low-risk zones.

Floodplain

- Part of every watershed
- Dry or semi-dry land area where water collects when it rains.
- Typically found near rivers, lakes, coasts and depressions
- Provides temporary natural storage for runoff
- Serves as recharge areas for the aquifer
- Provides important natural habitats for animals and plants

Floodway (Regulatory Floodway)

- The channel of a river or other water course and the adjacent land areas that must be reserved in order to discharge the base flood without cumulatively increasing the water surface elevation more than one foot.

LOMA (Letter of Map Amendment**)**
- An official amendment of a current Flood Insurance Rate Map (FIRM) accepted by FEMA for a property or a structure that verifies that the structure or portions of the property have been removed from a designated-floodplain area

ERODIBLE STREAM CHANNELS

Gully — Narrow ravine; hollow worn in the earth by a current of water
Gut — Narrow passage or gully as of a stream or path
Ravine — Long, narrow, deep gully or hollow in the earth's surface, worn by a stream or flood of water

WATERSHED

- An ecosystem
- Consist of three major components, stream channel, floodplain, and upland areas, that function together and drain to water bodies, including lakes, rivers, estuaries, wetlands, streams, and the surrounding landscape (groundwater recharge areas are also considered).
- Terms like catchment or drainage basin are also used to refer to watersheds.
  - Examples: Portion of a yard draining into a mud puddle, Mississippi River Basin

CONCEPTS

Aquifer — A geologic formation that stores, transmits, and yields significant quantities of water to wells and springs. The term **water-bearing** is sometimes used synonymously with aquifer when a stratum furnishes water for a specific use
Best Management Practice — Structural, vegetative, or managerial practices used to protect and improve our surface waters and groundwater
Slough (also spelled slew, slue) — A swamp, bog or marsh, especially one that is part of an inlet or backwater
Tufa — A porous rock formed as a deposit from springs or streams.

Urban Planning

Urban planning is the science of managing and directing city growth.

URBAN SPACES

Of, relating to, characteristic of, or constituting a city.

- Public spaces: Traditional street and square in a city
- Semi-Public: Shopping center, some managed children's play spaces
- Semi-Private Space: A front garden
- Private Space: Gardens or service yards

QUALITY OF LIFE FACTORS

- Climate and natural features
- Schools
- Housing
- Employment opportunities
- Medical facilities
- Cultural and recreational amenities
- Public services

CHARACTERISTICS OF SUCCESSFUL URBAN REGIONS

- Availability of water and food
- Health, transport, habitat, education, public services, public space, work, culture, leisure and a long life
- Protection of the environment
- Sustainable and equitable urban development, as well as environmentally and socially balanced urban planning
- Balanced maintenance and control of the land use
- Community participation
- An assurance of the right to association, assembly, expression and the democratic use of public space

INFORMATION USEFUL TO PLANNERS

- Trees—species, canopy cover, and area (or ecological community)
- Roads—primary, secondary, and tertiary
- Hydrograph—rivers, streams, lakes, reservoirs, etc.
- Census data—boundary lines and tabular data
- Wetlands—description of ecological area in a form useful to resource managers
- Farmland classifications—primary, secondary, etc.
- Physical geography information—slope, contour, elevation, aspect
- Rare and endangered species—nesting sites, range, etc.
- Soil types
- Vegetation types

NEW URBANISM

Neighborhood design trend used to promote community and livability. Characteristics include narrow streets, wide sidewalks, porches, and homes located closer together than typical suburban designs.

LANDSCAPE PLANNING

- Couple consideration of land suitability for urban uses with consideration of community goals and projected growth.
- Conserve natural areas to the extent possible
- Maximize natural water storage and infiltration opportunities
- Protect slopes and channels.

Wetlands

Areas that are frequently inundated or saturated with water for periods of time long enough to support vegetation suited for survival in saturated soils are classified as wetlands. Wetlands are natural pollution filters and flood valves

CLASSIFICATIONS

The various terms for a wetland are used interchangeably and with regional variations in the preferred word.

Bog

- An area having a wet, spongy, acidic substrate (soil) composed chiefly of sphagnum moss and peat in which characteristic shrubs and herbs and sometimes trees grow
- Has organic soil, unlike other wetlands, which have mineral soils
- Receive their water from precipitation.

Estuaries

- The part of the wide lower course of a river where its current is met by the tides.
- An arm of the sea that extends inland to meet the mouth of a river
- An estuary has somewhat salty water and tidal activity.

Fen

- Low marshy ground containing peat that is relatively rich in mineral salts and is alkaline rather than acidic
- Usually found in the upper parts of old estuaries or around fresh water lakes, with vegetation quite different from that of moors.

Marsh

- An area of soft, wet, low-lying land, characterized by grassy vegetation and often forming a transition zone between water and land
- Periodically wet or continually flooded area with the surface not deeply submerged.
- Covered dominantly with sedges, cattails, rushes, or other hydrophytic plants. Subclasses include freshwater and saltwater marshes.
- All marshes share two features in common:
  - All marshes contain vegetation that is not woody.
  - They tend to develop in zones progressing from terrestrial habitat to open water.

Swamp

- A forested or shrub-scrub wetland, contrasting with a marsh that has non-woody plants

- 108 -

CREATING AND MANAGING WETLANDS

Objectives
- To restore and enhancing existing wetland habitat types to prevent a net loss of functional and habitat values;
- To preserve and/or create particular wetland habitat types for specific desirable, threatened, or endangered species
- To consolidate many small compensation projects into one site;
- To balance wetland protection and development interests;
- To preserve bank wetlands in perpetuity through acquisition (or other preservation method), long-term monitoring and management
- to promote cooperation and administration among the various regulatory authorities

Factors to be considered
- Size and shape
- Proper watershed management
- Prevention of or appropriate application of disturbance
  - Examples: (Tillage, cutting, and burning) Erosion and sedimentation
- Pollution
  - Example: Herbicides and insecticides, heavy metals, sewage effluent-organic matter, livestock excrement, or raw sewage entering the water in large quantities depletes oxygen as it decomposes
- Plant-species diversity
  - Example: Invasive exotic and aggressive native plants
- Successional stage
  - Example: Local adapted native aquatic plants.
- Structural components
  - Examples: Excavation or filling or removing stream obstructions

Protection of watershed
- Installing terraces
- Practicing contour farming and minimizing or eliminating tillage on erodible, land; growing permanent perennial cover on steep hillsides
- Protecting riparian habitat (the zone flanking rivers and streams)
- Installing filter strips

Pollutant/effect
- Organic matter depletes oxygen from the water stressing or suffocating aquatic life
- Excess nutrients (nitrates, phosphorous) over stimulates the grown of algae depleting oxygen and harming aquatic life
- Acid precipitation harms or kills aquatic life
- Silt and suspended particles harms aquatic habitat
- Thermal pollution reduces oxygen and decomposition of organic matter which may shift species composition

Graphic Communication

Graphic communication is the process and art of combining text and graphics and communicating an effective message in the design. Today desktop publishing software and techniques are often used to achieve this goal.

Graphic Techniques

TYPES OF DRAWINGS

Orthographic drawings
- Three-dimensional objects represented by separate views arranged in a standard manner
- Called working drawings, or detailed drawings
- Used to show floor plans, elevations and sections
- Drawn to scale

Paraline drawings
- Includes all parallel line drawing types
- Three commonly used types:
  - **Isometric**
    - All planes receive equal emphasis.
  - **Diametric**
  - **Oblique**
    - Shows one face of the object in true shape, but the other faces on a distorted angle

Axonometric drawings
- Set of three or more views in which the object appears to be rotated at an angle, so that more than one side is seen
- Three-dimensional
- Can be used for the exact measuring of an object
- Types:
  - **Isometric**
    - Method of graphic representation of three-dimensional objects
    - Used to draw details, millwork, furniture and other design objects as well as buildings and interior rooms
    - Gives the appearance of viewing the object from one corner
    - Shows lines in their true length, but not all right angles are shown as such
  - **Dimetric**
    - Equally foreshortens 2 of the principal axes
  - **Trimetric**
    - Foreshortens all 3 of the principal axes

Perspective
- A kind of pictorial drawing that shows objects as they look to the eye

Diagram
- Plan, sketch, drawing, or outline designed to demonstrate or explain how something works or to clarify the relationship between the parts of a whole
- Allows one to graphically represent the idea of how things relate to each other.

Model
- Three-dimensional, physical construction of either an idea about a form or of an already drawn form
- To build a physical object that represents or investigates that thing
- Another means of description/inquiry.

Schematic
- Diagram using symbols, icons, and connecting lines

Pencil/ Ink drawings
- Line weight variation is determined by the 'weight' of the lead being used from light to dark
- Determined by the width of the drawn line from thin to thick
- Varies according to the type of drawing (plans, sections)
  - **Primary lines** (cuts/profiles) should be heaviest (widest)
  - **Secondary lines** (internal divisions, details) should be narrower
  - **Minor lines** (regulating lines/construction lines) should be lightest.
    - In axonometric drawings, lines that describe edges seen against space are the darkest.
    - Lines that describe changes in plane or surface conditions are lighter.

Proportion
- Considered in relation to the whole
- Relationship between things or parts of things with respect to comparative magnitude, quantity, or degree

Scale
- Proportion that the illustration of an object bears to the object itself

Bubble diagrams
- Used to define spaces within the landscape
- Frequently defined by the function that will take place in them
- Have many shapes and sizes

GRAPHIC COMPONENTS

Line quality
- Refers to consistency of a drawn line
- Has a consistent tone and weight

Line type

- **Dashed (hidden)** _ _ _ _ _ _ _ _ _ _
  - Denotes either a line that is obscured from view by another plane, or, a line that occurs in front of the picture plane
  - Shows important but invisible lines (medium)

- **Continuous line** _____
  - **Thick (bold)**
    - Visible outlines
  - **Thin**
    - Fictitious outlines
    - Imaginary intersection of surfaces
    - Dimension lines, projection lines, intersection lines and leaders
    - Hatching
    - Outlines of resolved sections
    - Adjacent parts and tooling
    - Fold and tangent bend lines
    - Short centerlines
  - **Thin, freehand or ruled with zig**
    - Indication of repeated detail
    - Break lines (other than on an axis)

- **Chain**
  - **Thin**
    - Centerlines
    - Pitch lines
    - Alternative position of moving part
    - Path lines for indicating movement
    - Features in front of a cutting plane
    - Developed views
    - Material to be removed
  - **Thick at ends and at change of direction, thin elsewhere**
    - Cutting planes
  - **Thick**
    - Indication of surfaces to meet special requirements

- **Center line** ____ _ ____ _ ____
  - Used to dimension to the center of arcs, circles, etc. (thin).

- **Phantom** ____ _ _ ____ _ _ ___
  - Used to indicate where cuts are made for section representations and used to show motion or travel of machine parts, etc. (thin).

- **Dimension lines**
  - Used to indicate length (thin), size, angles, etc. and includes a number and terminators (arrows or ticks).

- **Leader lines**
  - Used to label things (thin like dimension lines)
  - Includes a terminator arrow
  - Always horizontal near text
  - Always bent to diagonal near object

- **Extension lines**
  - Used to extend from object to dimension line (thin)
  - Must never touch object - leaving a visible gap to avoid confusing object with specification note (dimension)
  - Plan to avoid crossing other extension lines and/or dimension lines.

- **Break lines (thin)**
  - Straight with a zig-zag-zig
  - Used to omit portions of an object

- **Regulating lines**
  - Lines drawn in order to construct or regulate other lines
  - These are usually the first lines drawn, and are drawn lightly since their sole purpose is to serve as reference lines in the construction of a drawing.

Line weight
- Distinguishes between line types according to their 'weight"
- Dependent on the media being used

Subtraction
- Use of regulating lines to inform the removal of a portion of a solid volume

Extrusion
- Projection of regulating lines through a volume, so that the regulating lines "shave" parts of the volume away
- Similar to subtraction

Documentation

COVER SHEET

Serves as the title page
It should contain the following:
- Name of the company, company address, company phone number (include area code), logo (if you have one)
- Project name
- Names, addresses, phone numbers (include area code) of client
- Property legal description
- Vicinity map
- Date
- Consultants

AGREEMENT

Main document used to signify and formalize the construction contract between the Owner and Contractor
- Good agreement is divided into sections called Articles and are numbered consecutively.
- Standard Articles define the terms of the Agreement and establish the contractual obligations for each party
  - Work
  - Engineer/Architect
  - Contract Time
  - Monetary damages for delayed work completion
  - Contractor's price as defined in the bid
  - Payment Procedures
  - General Conditions

GENERAL CONDITIONS

- Legal standards that have been established to promote fair and objective contractual stipulations between all parties involved in construction projects
- Prepared with the advice of legal counsel and experienced professionals.
- Articles contained in the General Conditions describe the legal rights, responsibilities and contractual requirements of the Owner, Contractor, and Engineer
- Should only be modified with the help of legal counsel

Note: Technical information pertaining to how the project is to be constructed is not part of the GC's

ORGANIZATIONAL FORMAT

- **CSI MasterFormat™**
  - Used throughout the construction industry to format construction specifications in building contracts
  - Organized in a standardized outline form
  - Within 16 divisions are a number of sections. Each section is divided into three within each sections are parts—"general," "products," and "execution."
  - Within parts are articles and paragraphs.

TECHNICAL SPECIFICIATIONS

- Provides the Contractor with guidelines to follow during construction in conjunction with the project design supplements working drawing)
- Does not dictate to the Contractor how to install
- Includes a narrative list of materials, methods, model numbers, colors, allowances, and other details which supplement the information contained in the blue prints.

MAIN TYPES OF CONSTRUCTION SPECIFICATIONS

Written specifications are detailed presentation of a plan or proposal including all important and necessary criteria. Specifications prevail over drawing.

Prescription or closed specification
- Identifies the finished products and materials by brand name (Proprietary)
- Most restrictive as it does not allow for competitive bidding
- Limits product choice which can increase job cost
- Means 1 product or equal substitution allowed
- Requires approval by LA to ensure that product alternative meet standards

Performance or open specification
- Method of allowing as much choice as possible in the selection of finished products and materials by describing the end result required.

Descriptive
- Specifically describes the requirements for products and materials but not the manufacturers name (Reference Standard)
- Requires that the products and materials meet industry standards
- Reduces liability

Pure Performance
- Defines the specific criteria and results to be achieved for the construction products and materials
- Encourages creativity for construction components
- No often used as it is difficult to write and measure

Base-Bid
- Limits choice to select manufacturers
- Meets the requirements of public works
- Allows substitution with "approved equal"

MATERIAL LISTS

- A chart accompanying a project that details every part by letter, name, dimensions, material, and quantity
- May include notes that indicate special cutting instructions and finishes to be incorporated in the construction

ADDENDA (ADDENDUM)

- An agreement or list that is added to a contract, agreement, or other document such as a letter of intent after the original contract is signed
- Addresses changes or modifications made to the contract and issued prior to the bidding process
- Once issued, an addendum becomes part of the Contract Documents and supersedes the information that it modifies, adds or deletes.
- Will often facilitate adjustment to a Contractor's bid

SUBMITTALS

- Items that the contractor must submit for review and approval including such as, shop drawings, product data, samples, mock-ups, etc.
- Often prepared by subcontractors, vendors and material suppliers
- Must be reviewed, verified, approved, and signed by contractor
- Types:
  - **Shop Drawings**
    - Detailed drawings showing how building elements will be fabricated, usually prepared by the fabricator or manufacturer.
    - Provided in sufficient detail to indicate that the contractor intends to construct the referenced work in a manner that is consistent with the design intent and the contract documents
  - **Project data**
    - Refers to information that illustrates some portion of the work
    - Includes brochures, performance data, catalog pages, etc

CONSTRUCTION (FIELD WORK)

Fieldwork is the actual construction of the project. Field work includes the following.

Building Permits
- Must be issued before construction can begin
- Must provide the municipality's building department specifications and blueprints with the application for a permit.

- May be required to submit results of soil testing, environmental impact studies, and any other necessary testing or studies
- May require a public hearing if there is opposition to the project
- Usually issued within a few months or longer
- Paid for by either the owner or the general contractor
- Requires that a building inspector periodically verify that the project is being constructed according to applicable code

Subcontractors
- Range from a one-man operation to nationwide, publicly traded corporations, or divisions of larger corporations.
- Distinguished from general contractors by their limited scope of work
- Usually involves a special skill, knowledge, or ability
- Include plumbers, electricians, framers, and concrete workers
- Generally enter into contracts with the general contractor
- May provide the raw materials used in their specialty areas.
- Is paid by the general contractor, not the owner of the property
- Usually have purchased materials delivered directly to the job site
- May complete work in stages or be continuous

Scheduling of Subcontractors
- Responsibility of the general contractor
- Must schedule so that the subcontractor's work on the construction runs smoothly and completed on schedule.
- Must schedule in such a way that one subcontractor does not hold up another.
  - **Critical path**
    - Order on subcontractor sequencing

Working drawings
- Includes enough detail to show the general contractor the overall layout of the building.

Shop drawings
- Details the specific building components
- Produced by the individual specialty trades and suppliers from working drawings
- Includes items such as granite finishing, cabinets and countertops, structural steel, etc.
- Usually produced after the final design phase but before the beginning of the construction phase
- Prepared in accordance with the instructions on Document A201

Note: The role of the architect/engineer is to check each shop drawing for precise measurements and for compliance with the intended building design.

Submissions

- Illustrates each building item's intended use, function, method of attachment or installation requirements, and placed-in-service date
- Must receive the architect's approval to ensure that the item or product is in conformance with technical specifications

Note: The role of the architect and /or engineer is to monitor the contractor's progress, approves the progress payments made to the contractors and make modifications to the building plans as needed.

Change Orders

- Written contract revisions that increase or decrease the total contract price
- Contains the change order number, change order date, a description of the change, and the amount of the change order
- May be issued by contractors if stated in the contract

Construction Materials and Methods

Aggregates

Any hard, inert, mineral material used for mixing in graduated fragments. It includes sand, gravel, crushed stone, and slag.

USES

- As compacted aggregates in bases, subbases and shoulders for highways, walkways, airport runways, parking lots and railroads
  - **Coarser** aggregates are used for the base of the pavement structure
  - **Finer** aggregates for the surface or wearing course depending on lift thickness.
- As an aids in water filtration, purification and erosion control;
- As raw material used in combination with other resources to construct
  - Bridges
  - Schools and hospitals
  - Houses and apartments;
  - Commercial buildings and retail space;
  - Sewer systems
- As ingredients in hot mix asphalt
- As ingredients in Portland cement concrete.
- As special backfill material, riprap, mineral filler

MOHs HARDNESS SCALE

In mineralogy, hardness is defined as the resistance of the smooth surface of a mineral to scratching. It is determined by the Mohs scale of hardness. In the Mohs scale, ten common minerals are arranged in order of increasing hardness and assigned numbers

- Talc 1
- Gypsum 2 (fingernail at 2.5)
- Calcite 3 (copper (old penny) at 3.5)
- Fluorite, 4
- Apatite 5 (window glass or typical knife blade at under 5.5)
- Orthoclase 6 (streak plate or good steel file at over 6.5)
- Quartz 7
- Topaz 8
- Corundum 9
- Diamond 10 (Used in jewelry and cutting tools)

HARDNESS OF AGGREGATE

There are many different types of rock used as aggregate. The Mohs scale is used to measure the hardness of aggregate and has a range of 1-10. Most aggregates fall into the 2-9 range:

Mohs Range	Description	Aggregates
8-9	Critically Hard	Flint, Chert, Trap Rock, Basalt
6-7	Hard	River Rock, Granites, Quartz, Trap Rock
4-5	Medium/Hard	Granites, River Rock
3-4	Medium	Limestone, Sand Stone, Dolomite, Marble
2-3	Soft	Soft Limestone

AGGREGATES FOR PORTLAND CEMENT CONCRETE

Aggregates account for 60% to 75% of the total volume of concrete

Characteristics
- Clean
- Strength (stand up to pulling or crushing forces)
  - Affected by
    - Properties and proportions of the constituent materials
    - Degree of hydration
    - Rate of loading
  - Abrasion resistance
    - Direct function of its strength, and thus its water-cement ratio and constituent materials
    - Produce with high quality paste and strong aggregates
- Hardness
  - Controls the resistance of the aggregate to abrasion and degradation
    - Example: Weak particles have poor cementation.
- Physically and chemically stable
  - Strong particles free of absorbed chemicals or coatings of clay and other fine materials that could cause the deterioration of concrete
- Size, distribution, and interconnection of voids within individual particles
- Surface character and texture of the particles
- Gradation of the coarse and fine aggregates
- Mineral composition of the particles
- Particle shape
- Water absorption

Structures
- Rigid-pavement slabs
- Bridges
- Concrete barriers
- Sidewalks
- Curbs and backstop posts
- Slope walls

GRADED GRAVELS (GRADATIONS)

- The description given to the proportions of aggregate on a series of sieves
- Usually defined in terms of the % passing successive
- Best structural fill materials because they have a bridging factor that allows them to spread out over poor bearing soils

Examples include:
- **Baserock**
  - Well-graded aggregate suitable for compacting to such a degree that it provides a firm, stable base
  - Project specifications determine what class of aggregate base will be used.

- **Blend of -½" gravel**
  - Used for top dressing driveways and parking lots, drainage, and for solid foundations and structural backfill. It is also used in asphalt and concrete mixes.

- **Blend of -1" gravel**
  - Used for structural backfill and drainage.

- **Blend of -1½" gravel**
  - Used for top dressing driveways and parking lots, drainage, and for solid foundations and structural backfill
  - Also used in asphalt and concrete mixes.

- **Coarse Aggregate**
  - Consists of at least 90% by weight retained on the No. 4 sieve (⅜"(9.5mm) sieve)
  - Generally range between ⅜ and 1½" (9.5 mm to 37.5 mm) in diameter
  - Gravels and crushed stone

- **Crushed Aggregates**
  - Any hard, sound rock that is produced by blasting and then crushing. The aggregate is then screened to a specific size.

- **Dense-graded aggregate base (DGA)**
  - Mixture of primarily sand and gravel, well-graded from coarse to fine (usually unstabilized, but sometimes asphalt or cement stabilized).

- **Drainage aggregate**
  - Open-graded aggregate with high permeability.

- **Fine Aggregate**
  - Consists of at least 90% by weight passing the No. 4 sieve
  - Generally consist of natural sand or crushed stone

- **Landscape Rock**
  - Variety of sizes from 6" – 12" in diameter

- **#5 Gravel**
  - Larger gravel measuring roughly 1½"
  - Used as fill for septic tanks, back fill, and more.

- **#8 Gravel**
  - Smaller than the #5 gravel measuring ¾" mid-sized rough gravel
  - Used in making concrete, back fills, landscaping

- **Oversize Gravel**
  - Larger rough gravel
  - Primarily used for roadways as a base or as a fill on larger projects
  - Sometimes used for commercial landscaping projects.

- **Oversize Stone**
  - Washed, it is a blend of -6" gravel
  - Used for solid fill, drainage, and wash-out retention.

- **Pea Gravel**
  - Smooth and rounded stone
  - Sized at ⅜" and down
  - Typically used in drainage applications, in PCC, landscaping, as a fill under slab, for roofing

- **Pit Run**
  - Compactable filling material
  - Mixture of filling dirt with gravel
  - Used mostly for base filling under large areas where some rock needs to be in place but saves on cost in using just gravel.

- **Stabilized aggregate:**
  - Aggregate that contains an asphaltic or cement binder

SAND

The component of the mix which determines the abrasiveness of the concrete
Can either be "sharp" (abrasive) or "round" (non-abrasive).

- **#23-24 Sand**
  - Used primarily for asphalt and concrete in the making of state highways and interstates.

- **Fill Sand**
  - Used mostly for the sub-base for concrete slab
  - Does not continue to depress over time
  - Excellent material for foundation fills.

- **Mason Sand**
  - Fine grade of sand that is primarily used in concrete mortar

Asphalt Construction

Asphalt pavement refers to any paved road surfaced with asphalt. Hot Mix Asphalt (HMA) is a combination of approximately 95% stone, sand, or gravel bound together by asphalt cement, a product of crude oil.

ADVANTAGES

- Easy to keep free of snow and ice in the winter
- Not affected by ice control chemicals
- Relatively dirt-free in the summer
- Economical
- Durable
- Long lasting (virtually trouble free service for up to 20 years)
- Require minimal maintenance
- May be colored and patterned
- Versatile
  - Can be designed to handle virtually any traffic loading, soils and materials
  - Can be used to salvage old pavements as well as to build new ones
  - Phased construction can easily be incorporated.
- Can be constructed rapidly
- Ready for immediate use
- Can be recycled
- Minimizes traffic noise
- Allows pavement striping to be highly visible on the black surface.
- Flexible-type pavement.

HOT MIX ASPHALT

- **Asphalt "binder" (asphalt cement)**
  - Liquid asphalt cement
  - Material that coats the aggregate particles and acts as the glue that holds the mix together

- **Aggregates**
  - Provide the structure and framework that gives an asphalt mixture its stability and strength.
  - May consist of:
    - **Natural** aggregate (river gravel and sands)
    - **Processed** aggregates (from quarry and blasting operations)

- **Air voids in the mixture**
  - Controlled through the aggregate gradation and the quantity of liquid asphalt
  - Determined prior to construction (during the mix design phase) in order for the mixture to have the desired properties

BASE (BASE COURSE)

A layer or layers of specified or selected granular material of designed thickness, constructed on the subgrade or subbase for the purpose of supporting the pavement by distributing load, providing drainage, and/or minimizing frost action.

- May be composed of crushed stone; crushed slag; crushed or uncrushed gravel and sand; or combinations of these materials
- May be bound with asphalt (asphalt base course)

TYPICAL BASE DESIGNATIONS

- 25 MM Superpave
  - Generally a minimum lift thickness of 4" is recommended
- 19 MM Superpave (HL-8 mix)
  - Generally a minimum lift thickness of 3" is recommended
  - Often used as the base course
- 12.5 MM Superpave (HL-3 mix)
  - Generally a minimum lift thickness of 2" is recommended
  - Driveway mixes

TYPICAL SURFACE DESIGNATIONS

- 12.5 MM Superpave
  - Has a high stability designed for use on roadways with:
    - Average Daily Traffic (ADT)—greater than 15,000
    - Recommended minimum lift thickness 2"
    - Used for roads and parking lots
- 9.5 MM Superpave
  - Recommended for most surface applications.
  - Recommended minimum lift thickness 1½"
- 4.75 MM Superpave
  - Primarily for thin lift leveling or correcting minor deviations
  - Fine mix that can be placed in lifts as thin as ½".

PAVEMENT DESIGN

The weight and volume of the heaviest traffic is a principal factor in pavement design. Typical pavement sections include the following:

- **Residential Drive**
  - Essentially limited to passenger cars
- **Parking Lots & Residential or Light Duty Streets**
  - Present and future traffic limited to passenger cars plus normal service trucks.
- **Minor Arterial & Light Industrial Streets**
  - Present and future traffic limited to a medium duty classification which includes some heavy truck and bus traffic
- **Principal Arterial, Commercial or Industrial Roads**
  - Present and future traffic is a heavy duty classification

RECOMMENDED MIXES FOR NORMAL HMA APPLICATIONS

Traffic Designation	Equivalent Single Axle Loading	Typical Roadway Applications
Low	< 300,000 ESAL's	Light traffic volumes, local, special roadways serving recreational sites
Moderate	300,000 to < 10,000,000 ESAL's	Most local roadways, state routes, US Highways,
High	>10,000,000 ESAL's	Multilane, Highly trafficked, truck climbing lanes

PERPETUAL PAVEMENT

The name coined to describe a three-layer, flexible pavement design and construction concept.
- Produces a deep-strength asphalt pavement that can resist structural fatigue distress indefinitely (more than 50 years)
- Can be economically maintained by replacing just the surface

SUPERPAVE

System of material specifications and laboratory mix design methods based on performance criteria developed under the Strategic Highway Research Program (SHRP).
Designed to reliably perform under any loading or environmental conditions

DRAINAGE

Proper drainage is essential to the success of hot mix asphalt pavements. Water in pavement systems is one of the principal causes of pavement distress. Wet soils or aggregates are not as strong as dry soils or aggregates under most circumstances.
- **Subsurface drainage**
  - Required where high water tables occur or where water may accumulate in low areas
  - Underdrains and/or interceptor drains required to prevent the accumulation of water beneath the pavement structure.
- **Surface drainage**
  - A minimum slope or crown of 1.5% per foot is recommended.
  - The roadway shoulder or adjacent ground should be graded so that surface drainage runs away from the pavement and does not stand on the pavement's edge.

Note: On large parking lots, sloped sections, catch basins, and storm drains may be necessary for proper drainage.

TYPICAL DRAINABLE PAVEMENT

- **Surface Pavement**
  All elements from the wearing surface of a roadway to the subgrade: Surface pavement (asphalt or PCC), base (may include permeable base), and subbase. **Rigid**: Portland Cement Concrete
  o **Flexible**: Asphaltic Concrete

- **Permeable Base**
  o A free draining layer in the pavement designed to rapidly remove free water from most elements of pavement.
  o Usually placed between the surface of the pavement and a separator/filter layer
  o **Unstablized** Granular
  o **Asphalt** Stabilized Granular
  o **Cement** Stabilized Granular

- **Separator/Filter Layer (aggregate or geotextile)**
  o A geotextile or aggregate (subbase) layer separating a permeable base layer from an adjacent soil (or aggregate) containing fines to prevent the fines from contaminating the drainage aggregate.

- **Subgrade**
  o Foundation for the asphalt pavement structure

- **Edgedrains**
  o A subsurface drain usually located at the edge of the pavement (between the asphalt and shoulder) at an appropriate depth to intercept expected pavement section infiltration water.
  o Aggregate Trench Drain w/ Geotextile (including outlets with headwalls) Filter & Pipe
  o Prefabricated Geocomposite Edgedrain (PGED)

- **Shoulders**
  o The portion of the roadway contiguous with the traveled way for accommodation of stopped vehicles, for emergency use
  o Provides lateral support of base and surface courses
  o Sloped

DRIVEWAYS

Subgrade
- Must be smooth, firm, and even
- Contour to match the layout of the drive
- Free of organic material and topsoil.
- Use between 6" (150mm) and 8" (200mm) of properly compacted crushed granular base aggregate on top of the subgrade to aid in water filtration, purification and erosion control

Pavement

- Minimum compacted thickness of 2" (50mm) of hot mix asphalt.
- For a more durable driveway a 2" (50mm) HMA base course followed by a 1.5" (40mm) surface course.
- Note: As a rule of thumb the compacted thickness of each asphalt layer is typically about three quarters the thickness of loose hot asphalt mix.

Drainage

- Should have a slope from crown to edge - typically ¼" per foot (2 cms for each meter of width).
- An 18" (460mm) fall is recommended for every 100" (30 meters) of driveway.
- Must be away from buildings
- Must not allow water to rest on the edges of the pavement
- Underdrains are not usually needed

DRIVE WAY CONSTRUCTION

Subgrade (Smooth and firm)
- Remove soft areas and repair with compacted crushed aggregate.
- Spread and compact granular base to a uniform thickness

Hot mix asphalt (must arrive at the proper temperature)
- Too hot (look for blue smoke) will cause some surface raveling and possible premature hardening
- Too cold will not compact properly.
- For best results, pave when the weather is warm and dry.

Placement of HMA
- Should not lay down more than 2" (5cm) of compacted asphalt hot mix in a single lift.
- Avoid hand placement of the asphalt hot mix.

Rolling and compaction

- Start as soon as the hot mix asphalt can be compacted without displacement
- Continue until the mix is thoroughly compacted and all roller marks have disappeared

ASPHALT RECYCLING

Twice as much asphalt pavement is recycled as paper, glass, plastic and aluminum combined.
- Reduces the use of virgin materials
- Helps to preserve landfill space
- Stretches tax dollars, allowing more roads to be kept in better condition

CONCEPTS

Base crossdrain — A subsurface drain, generally perpendicular to the roadway alignment, designed to drain infiltrated water. Often needed at bridge abutments and across the road on long downgrades

Bituminous Damp-proofing — Impregnated mixtures of hydrocarbons, like tar or asphalt, together with their nonmetallic derivatives used on a surface to prevent moisture from passing through

Drainage pipe — Rigid or flexible pipe conduit designed to collect and/or transport water out of the pavement section (usually perforated).

Headwall — A protective structure at an edge drain outlet

Outlet — Point of discharge of an edge drain

- May be the pipe or a headwall

Outlet pipe — The lateral connection from the edgedrain to the outlet

- Usually a solid pipe
- Usually strong to prevent damage

Prefabricated geocomposite edge drain (PGED) — An edge drain consisting of a drainage core covered with geotextile.

- Usually 1 - 2" thick by 1 – 3' high, placed in a narrow trench
- May include drainage aggregate or sand

Self-Adhering Membrane — A membrane that can adhere to a substrate and to itself at overlaps without the use of an additional adhesive

Subbase — Layer or layers of specified or selected material of designed thickness
Placed on a subgrade to support a base course

Tar — Brown or black bituminous material, liquid or semi-solid in consistency, in which the predominating constituents are bitumens obtained as condensates in the processing of coal, petroleum, oil-shale, wood, or other organic materials

Underdrain — Deep subsurface drain located at a sufficient depth to intercept and lower the ground water to a required design level.

Awnings and Canopies

CANOPIES

- Construct of a metal framework with an approved covering, that is flame resistant as determined by both the small-scale and large-scale tests in accordance with NFPA 701 or that has a flame spread rating not greater than 25 when tested in accordance with ASTM E84
- Use only flame resistant textile covering for the canopy
- Have a flame spread index not greater than 25 when tested in accordance with ASTM E 84 in the form intended for use any canopy covering, other than textiles
- Attach canopies to the building at the inner end and supported at the outer end by not less than two stanchions, with braces anchored in an approved manner.
- Place stanchions not less than 44" (1118 mm) apart.

- Not have the horizontal portion of the framework less than 8' (2438 mm) nor more than 12' (3658 mm) above the walking surface and the clearance between the covering or valance and the walking surface shall not be less than 7' (2134 mm)
- Have at least one long side open

RETRACABLE AWNING

Cover with a frame that retracts against a building or other structure to which it is entirely supported.

- Design and construct to withstand wind or other lateral loads and live loads with due allowance for shape, open construction and similar features that relieve the pressures or loads.
- Protect structural members to prevent deterioration.
- Have awning frames of noncombustible material, fire-retardant-treated wood, wood of Type IV size, or 1-hour construction with combustible or noncombustible covers and shall be fixed, retractable, folding or collapsible.
- Construct canopies of a rigid framework with an approved covering that is flame resistant in accordance with NFPA 701 or has a flame spread index not greater than 25 when tested in accordance with ASTM E 84.

FLAGPOLE

Basic types
- External halyard flagpoles
- Internal halyard
- Outrigger flagpoles
- Vertical wall mount flagpoles
- Nautical flagpoles
- Counter balanced flagpoles

Foundation Methods
- Ground Set: Setting the pole into the ground
- Shoe Base: Fasten the pole to a concrete pad
- Wall mount

Materials
- Aluminum
- Bronze
- Stainless-steel
- Steel
- Fiberglass

Chain Link Fences and Gates

CHAIN LINK FABRIC

The fabric is formed by weaving a series of spirals together

Gauge
- Standard mill diameter tolerance is + or - .005".
- Common gauges and diameters:
  - 6 gauge=.192"
  - 9 gauge=.148"
  - 11 gauge=.120"
  - 11 ½ gauge=.113"
  - 12 gauge=.106"
  - 12 ½ gauge=.099

Height
- Available in heights of 36", 42", 48", 60", 72", 84", 96", 120", and 144".

Selvage
- How the top and bottom of fence is finished
  - Less than 72" must knuckle both ends by industry standard (KK)
  - Heights of 72" and higher, are generally twisted or barbed at one end and knuckled (BK) on the other.
  - For high security enclosures, chain link can be obtained with both ends twisted or barbed (BB).

Zinc coatings
- Galvanized after weaving (G.A.W.)
- Galvanized before weaving (G.B.W

Mesh size
- Distance between two parallel wires in the fabric
- Most common mesh sizes are 2" or 2 ¼"
- Smaller meshes are available for projects that require a higher degree of security.

FRAME WORK

Tubular steel frame that chain link fabric is attached to

Components
- **Terminal posts**
  - Set in concrete and are end, corner, and gate posts.

- **Line posts**
  - Smaller in diameter than terminal posts
  - Intermediate posts between terminal posts
  - Set in concrete

- **Top rail**
  - o Attached to the terminal posts
  - o Passes through fittings, which are attached to line posts
  - o Provides a horizontal frame that supports that fabric

Coating (ASTM F669-92)
- **Hot dip process**
  - o Pipe dipped into a pot of molten zinc and submersed
  - o Interior and exterior of the pipe are zinc coated.
- **In-line flow coat galvanizing**
  - o Pipe passes through an in line vat of molten zinc which coats the exterior
  - o Clear organic coating is applied over the zinc to provide additional protection
  - o Interior of the tubing is coated with a zinc rich paint.

FITTINGS (ASTM F 626-96)

Types
- Those used in the line of fence,
- Those used on terminal posts
- Those used in conjunction with gates

Use
- **Residential**
  Made from a die cast aluminum or steel that has been galvanized
- **Industrial and commercial fittings**
  Made from galvanized steel, cast iron, or malleable steel

GATES

Residential applications
- **Single walk**
  - o Generally used for people to pass through (can be made up to 12')
  - o Same height as the fence
  - o Single panel that is hinged from one terminal post and latched to another
- **Double drive**
  - o Consist of two panels that latch in the middle of the opening.

Commercial projects
- **Single walk**
- **Double drive gates**
- **Sliding gates**
  - o Used where there is no room to swing the panel of a single or double gate.
- **Rolling gates**
  - o Roll on a pipe track that is attached by track brackets to the gate post and line posts and is on a ground carrier that is attached to the front of the gate
  - o Commercial single and double drive gates are usually welded, but can also be made with gate ells

GATE ACESSORIES

Select for adjoining fence and framework

Butt hinge
- The most common type
- When the door is closed, the two halves are folded tightly. Usually, one half is mortised into the doorframe while other the other is recessed in the stile. While ordinary steel butt hinges are cheap and durable, ball-bearing butt hinges move more smoothly and quietly.

Gate latch
- A fitting to hold the gate in place when closed

Latch set
- A set of door hardware comprising a latch, strike, spindle, and knob/lever
- Used to fasten a door closed and open the door by turning a knob/lever or operating a latch grip handle.
- Does not necessarily include a locking mechanism

Lockset
- A complete set of door hardware used for the entrance door or some other door requiring keyed entry
- Includes a lock mechanism; some type of knob, lever, pull, or latch grip handle; and other accessories

Strap Hinge
- For door hardware, a strap hinge is a hinge with at least one long strap that extends across the surface of the gate or door, often with rivets

Concrete Construction

Cement and concrete are often used interchangeably. Cement, a powder material, is one of the components used to make concrete. Concrete is a composition material consisting of Portland cement, aggregate, and water. When mixed together, this will result in a chemical action that will set and harden into rock-like mass.

CONCEPTS

Accelerator — Material used to speed up the setting of mortar

Admixtures — Chemical additives included in the mixing batch for concrete manufacture or applied to the surface during the curing or setting process of the concrete to accelerates or retard the curing time, provides coloring, waterproofing, tearing, special aggregate finishes, etc.

Aggregate — Coarse material, such as gravel, broken stone or sand, with which cement and water are mixed to form concrete, surfacing or ballasting
- Sand + cement paste = mortar
- Mortar + gravel = concrete

Air entrained (Aerated Concrete) — Concrete that has been altered chemically, with an additive, to disperse air bubbles through the mix.
- Easier to work than standard concrete
- Stands up well in cold weather
- Resists salts better than other concrete
- Not as strong as regular concrete

Binder — Controls the properties of the concrete
- It is the inclusion of water (hydration) into the product that causes concrete to set, stiffen, and become hard

Clinker — Product that is a mixture of compounds finely ground into powder form
Green concrete — Freshly poured concrete that has not yet cured
- Generally considered "green" for 8 to 48 hours after it has set

Hydration — The incorporation of water into a substance
- In the hydration of cement, chemical changes occur slowly, eventually creating new crystalline products, heat evolution, and other measurable signs

Plasticizer — An admixture used to increase the fluidity of fresh cement with the same cement/water ratio improving the workability and placement of the cement
Psi — Abbreviation for 'pounds per square inch
- Used to describe the desired compressive strength of the concrete with higher psi's meaning stronger concrete
- Most exterior residential concrete should be 4000 psi to help insure durability
- Conventional concrete has strengths of 7,000 psi or less;
- 3000psi means that it is strong enough to carry a compressive stress of 3,000 psi (20.7 MPa) at 28 days

Retarders — A chemical admixture to mortar or grout that slows setting or hardening times
Set — Process of water and cement forming a cement paste that begins to react and harden
- This paste binds the aggregate particles through the chemical process of hydration.
- Cement + water = hardened cement paste

Soil cement — A mixture of water, cement, and natural soil, usually processed in a tumble and mixed to a specific consistency, then placed in lifts and rolled to compact to provide slope protection.
Soil cement base — Consists of a mixture of the natural subgrade material and Portland cement in the proper amounts
- After thorough mixing, the proper amount of water is added, and the material is compacted to the required thickness.
-

Soil-cement linings — Are constructed with mixtures of sandy soil, cement and water, which harden to a concrete-like material
- The cement content should be from 2-8% of the soil by volume.

Stucco (Portland Cement Plaster) — Combination of Portland cement-based cementations material and sand mixed with a suitable amount of water to form a plastic mass
- Applied as a two-or-three part coating on flat or curved surfaces either inside or outside any building or structure

Vibrating screed — A machine designed to act as a vibrator while leveling freshly placed concrete
Vibration — Energetic agitation of freshly mixed concrete during placement by mechanical devices, either pneumatic or electric, that create vibratory impulses of moderately high frequency that assist in evenly distributing and consolidating the concrete in the formwork.
- **External vibration** employs a device attached to the forms and is particularly applicable to the manufacture of precast items and for the vibration of tunnel lining forms.
- **Internal vibration** employs an element which can be inserted into the concrete; and is more generally used for cast-in-place construction

Water — Key reactant in cement hydration
Waterstop — A synthetic rubber ribbon installed between concrete constructions joints to prevent the passage of water. Bentonite clay is also used as a water stop in substructural joints.
Yard of concrete — One cubic yard of concrete is 3' X 3' X 3' in volume, or 27 cubic feet. One cubic yard of concrete will pour 80 square feet of 3 ½" sidewalk or basement/garage floor.

COMMON TESTS FOR FRESH CONCRETE

Pressure meter — Test measures the air trapped within the mortar of the concrete mixture
Can be used on all types of concrete mixtures including ones containing porous aggregates, due to the fact that the results are not affected by the air contained in the aggregate
Chace Air Indicator — Simple and inexpensive way to check the approximate air content of freshly mixed concrete
Kelly Ball — A device for determining the consistency of fresh concrete
Sometimes used as an alternative to the slump test.
Schmidt (or Swiss) Hammer Test — This test gives an estimate of the concrete's compressive strength.
This test is performed in situations where the concrete has already been poured and a cylinder test is not possible.
Slump test — A measure of the consistency of plastic concrete relative to the amount it falls when a slump cone filled with concrete is lifted vertically. The slump cone is then placed beside the specimen of concrete and the number of inches from the top of the cone to the top of the specimen of concrete is the slump.

CEMENT

Gray powder that is the "glue" in concrete which hardens when mixed with water. It comprises from 10% to 15% of the concrete mix, by volume.

Cement mixtures

Mixtures are always listed as parts Cement to Sand to Aggregate. Following are typical cement mixtures description:

- **Rich**
  - 1 part cement, 2 parts sand, 3 parts coarse aggregate
  - Used for concrete roads and waterproof structures
- **Standard**
  - 1 part cement, 2 parts sand, 4 parts coarse aggregate
  - Used for reinforced work floors, roofs, columns, arches, tanks, sewers, conduits, etc.
- **Medium**
  - 1 part cement, 2½ parts sand, 5 parts coarse aggregate
  - Used for foundations, walls, abutments, piers, etc.
- **Lean**
  - 1 part cement, 3 parts sand, 6 parts coarse aggregate
  - Used for all mass concrete work, large foundations, backing for stone masonry, etc

Cement slurry

- A thin, watery cement mixture for pumping or for use as a wash over a surface

Cement types

- **Type I Normal**
  - General purpose cement suitable for practically all uses in residential construction
  - Should not be used where it will be in contact with high sulfate soils or be subject to excessive temperatures during curing
- **Type II Moderate**
  - Used where precaution against moderate sulfate attack is important, as in drainage structures where sulfate concentrations in groundwaters are higher than normal or when heat build-up is a concern
- **Type III High Early Strength**
  - Used when high strengths are desired at very early periods, usually a week or less. It is used when it is desirable to remove forms as soon as possible or to put the concrete into service quickly.
- **Type IV Low Heat**
  - For use where the amount and rate of heat generated during curing must be kept to a minimum. The development of strength is slow and is intended in large masses of concrete such as dams
- **Type V Sulfate Resisting**
  - For use only in construction exposed to severe sulfate action, such as western states having soils of high alkali content.
  - Resists chemical attack by soil and water high in sulfates
- **Types IA, IIA and IIIA**
  - Used to make air-entrained concrete
  - Have the same properties as Types I, II, and III, except has small quantities of air-entrained materials combined with them.

Portland cement

- A generic term referring to the finely powdered cement material

White cement

- Fits the characteristics of Type I or Type III, but manufactured so that the finished product is white.
- Used to make roofing tile, swimming pool plaster, , architectural panels, terrazzo surfaces, stucco, cement paint, and decorative grouts

CURING

Curing is the maintenance of a satisfactory moisture content and temperature in concrete during its early stages so that desired properties may develop. These properties include strength and durability.

- New concrete needs to be kept moist for 5 – 7 days after placement to cure properly
- Concrete takes approximately four weeks to cure to full strength (depending on the weather)

COMPRESSIVE STRENGTH

Concrete may vary greatly in compressive strength which is measured in POUNDS per SQUARE INCH (PSI).

Strength of the concrete

- The easiest way to add strength is to add cement
- Most influential factor in concrete strength is the ratio of water to cement in the cement paste (ratio ranges from 0.35 to 0.6) that binds the aggregates together
- Higher this ratio is, the weaker the concrete will be and vice versa.
- Every desirable physical property will be adversely affected by adding more water. This is due to the increase in porosity (space between particles) that is created with the hydration process.

Chart of hardness

Concrete Hardness	PSI	Application
Critically Hard	8,000 +	Nuclear power plants
Hard	6-8,000	Bridge piers
Medium	4-6,000	Highways
Soft	3,000 or less	Sidewalks & patios

REINFORCED CONCRETE

Reinforcement means adding steel to the concrete prior to pouring it into place.

Uses
- Any large surface for a room or patio should be reinforced.
- Any concrete wall
- Anything that will take a lot of weight, such as a driveway should be reinforced.
- Optional for sidewalks and decorative projects

Wire mesh
- Comes in rolls and can be rolled out to cover a large area quickly and easily
- The most common wire mesh is #10 with wire spacing of 6".
- Most commonly used reinforcement for all backyard projects.
- Serves as a means of increasing slab tensile strength

Rebar
- Used where heavier reinforcement is needed such as footings or tying the new slab into an existing slab
- Most bars are "deformed," a pattern is rolled onto them which help the concrete get a grip on the bar.
- Plain bars are also made, but are used only in special situations in which the bars are expected to slide (for example, crossing expansion joints in highway pavement)

Fiber Mesh
- Used in cast- in-place concrete applications such as slabs-on-grade to control plastic shrinkage cracking and reduce settlement shrinkage
- Used in various small precast concrete products and in stucco and mortar applications.

REBARS

- Rebar are ribbed steel bars installed in foundation concrete walls, footers, and poured in place concrete structures designed to strengthen concrete.
- Comes in various thicknesses and strength grade

Rebar Mat
- Simply means that rebar is tied in a mat with bars being placed 90º to each other. Spacing is usually called out as O.C. (on center) or Each Way.
  - Example: #4 Bars 6" O.C., would be ½" rebar placed in line 6" O.C., or 6" apart. Each Way means rebar tied in each direction at a specific spacing.
  - Example - # 4 Bar 6" each way, or ½" rebar tied on 6" centers, each way.

Rebar sizes and grades

Imperial bar designations represent the bar diameter in fractions of ⅛", such that #8 = 8/8 inch = 1" diameter.

Imperial Bar Size	"Soft" Metric Size	Weight (lbs/ft)	Nominal Diameter (in)	Nominal Diameter (mm)
#3	#10	0.376	0.375 (⅜")	9.525
#4	#13	0.668	0.500 (½)	12.7
#5	#16	1.043	0.625 (5/8")	15.875
#6	#19	1.502	0.750 (¾")	19.05
#7	#22	2.044	0.875 (⅞")	22.225
#8	#25	2.67	1 (1")	25.4

- The most common sizes are #3 (⅜"), #4 (½"), and #5 (5/8"). The overall diameter is about 1/16" larger than the nominal size, because the ribs and deformations project slightly. Half-inch rebar might fit a half-inch hole in thin material, but it might be a very tight fit.
- Grade 40 rebar is the most common for homes and landscaping;
- Grades 50 and 60 are harder and stronger.
- Rebar is usually sold in 20' lengths, but shorter lengths are available, or can be cut at the store.

Size	Examples
Light	Wire mesh, single mat.
Medium	#4 rebar, every 12" on center each way (OCEW) Single mat, Wiremesh, multi-mat
Heavy	#5 rebar, 12" OCEW, single mat. #4 rebar, 12" OCEW, double mat.

GEOGRIDS

Net-shaped synthetic polymer-coated fibers that are used to reinforce earth-fill slope, wall and base layer construction.

Factors that affect interlocking ability
- Geogrid strength
- Mesh size
- Base materials used

Applications
- **Slope Reinforcement**
  - Highway embankments, overpasses, or erosion-prone surfaces and landfill walls
- **Base Reinforcement**
  - Foundations for roads, parking lots, railroad track beds, airport tarmacs and runways
- **Wall Reinforcement**
  - Retaining walls, airport noise barriers, bridge supports and sea walls
- **Berm Reinforcement**
  - Spillway channels for earthen dams, levees and waste containment ponds

CONCRETE PLACEMENT

Architectural pre-cast concrete
- Designed for function, appearance and durability
- Plant cast, architecturally finished, pre-cast concrete units
- Includes panels, concrete countertops, benches, balustrade, pier caps, copings, sills, tables, fireplaces, flooring, and accent pieces
- Includes colors, stamped designs, exposed aggregate

Cast-in-place concrete (Sitecast)
- Concrete that is poured into forms that are erected at the job site.
- Most common type of concrete placement
- Same as the term site casting

Cast-in-place (Limited applications)
- Limited to small, simple, structurally noncritical concrete projects
- Used for residential, light-commercial, and light-retail building projects
- Includes footings, grade beams, slabs-on-grade, and basement or foundation walls without special structural requirements or finish treatments

Gunite
- Pneumatically applied (sprayed) concrete that is a dry mixture of cement, aggregate and/or sand.
- Water is applied to the mix at the hose nozzle.

Pre-cast concrete
- Cast into permanent shapes using reusable forms at a plant, then transported as fully cured structural units to the actual construction job site.
- See cast-in-place concrete.

Ready-mixed concrete (Transit-mixed)
- Batched or mixed at a central plant before it is delivered to a construction site and delivered ready for placement.
- Known as transit-mixed concrete since it is often transported in an agitator truck.

Shotcrete
- Process where concrete is projected or "shot" under pressure using a feeder or "gun" onto a surface to form structural shapes including walls, floors, and roofs
- Can be projected on wood, steel, polystyrene, or other surface
- Used in most cases as a structural material
- Can be trowelled smooth while the concrete is still wet

Tilt-up construction
- A method of constructing concrete walls in which the wall panels are cast and cured flat on the floor slab or surrounding area and then tilted up into their final wall positions.

CONCRETE CONTROL

The use of concrete is often divided as follows:

Large quantity-critical usage
- All pavement and structure concrete, and in general any other concrete usage exceeding 200 cubic yards (150 cubic meters) per day

Small quantity-noncritical usage
- Sidewalks - Not to exceed approximately 500 square yards (418 square meters) per day.
- Curbing, combination curb and gutter - Not to exceed approximately 500 linear feet (152 linear meters) per day.
- Patching and temporary pavements
- Building foundations and floors
- Slope paving and paved gutter
- Guardrail and fence post anchorages
- Metal pile castings
- Culvert headwalls
- Catch basins, manhole bases, and inlets
- Sign, signal, and light bases

DECORATIVE CONCRETE

Acid stain (or chemical stain)
A stain containing inorganic salts dissolved in an acidic, water-based solution that reacts chemically with the minerals in hardened concrete to produce permanent, transparent color that will not peel or flake. Gives concrete an attractive variegated or marbleized appearance. Colors tend to be earth tones, such as tans, browns, reddish browns, and greens. (Also see polymer stain).

Decorative aggregate — Richly colored natural stones, such as basalts, granite, quartz, or limestone, used to enhance exposed-aggregate concrete or decorative toppings.

Dyes — Translucent color solutions containing very fine pigments that penetrate into the concrete surface. Will not chemically react with concrete (like acid stains will)

Stamped concrete — Concrete flatwork that is patterned with platform tools, stamping mats, or seamless texturing skins to resemble materials such as brick, slate, stone, tile, and wood planking

Stenciled concrete — A decorative surface treatment using heavy-duty paper stencils with stone, tile, or brick patterns that are lightly pressed into fresh concrete, followed by the application of dry-shake color hardeners. When the stencils are removed, the uncolored concrete mimics mortar joints. Another technique, for use on existing concrete, is to apply adhesive stencils and then color, etch, or sandblast the surface.

Adhesive stencils — Adhesive-backed masking patterns made of vinyl/plastic used for creating stenciled concrete effects. The adhesive keeps the patterns firmly in place on the concrete surface while the decorative treatment of choice is applied, such as acid stains, dyes, spray-down systems, etching gels, or sandblasting.

MORTAR

Mortar is typically composed of cement, lime and sand. Components and proportions of mortars vary depending on the desired mortar properties. Mortars consisting of Portland cement and lime as well as sand are most common.

Function of mortar
- Bonding agent that integrates brick into a masonry assembly
- Helps to create a water resistant barrier
- Accommodates dimensional variations and physical properties of the brick
- Permits some movement between units
- Allows for the use of ties and reinforcing to the unit
- Enhances the aesthetics through color and texture

Characteristics
- Used as a joining medium in masonry, wood, or other materials, joining them into a unified mass
- Limited life- 1½ -2 hours
- Mixture gradually hardens when exposed to the air
- Must fill joint completely to create a watertight and strong wall

Types
- **Type N**
  - Used in general masonry walls above grade
  - Used in non-structural applications in new construction
  - Has good bond qualities and good resistance to water penetration.
  - Specifically recommended for parapets, chimneys and exterior walls subjected to severe weathering conditions for general re-pointing of walls
- **Type S**
  - Typically used in structural masonry applications
  - Recommended for use in masonry where maximum flexural strength is required for chimneys, parapets and load-bearing masonry constructions
- **Type M**
  - Typically used only in below grade applications.
- **Type 0**
  - Relatively low compressive strength mortar suitable for limited exterior use and general interior use in load bearing and non-load bearing masonry
  - Should not be used where it will be subject to freezing in the presence of moisture
  - For repointing of softer masonry or masonry where Type O mortar design mix was used

Thin-set
- Used to describe the installation of tile with all materials except Portland cement mortar, which is the only recognized thick-bed method
- Applied to subfloor (Thin-set mortar ⅛" (3 mm))
- Set same size stones generally ¼" (6 mm), ⅜" (10mm) on top
- Most suited for thin stones cut to same size
- Can be placed on either concrete or wood subfloors reinforced with a secondary layer of plywood, cement backer board, or for a more durable application

Thick-set
- Used to describe a thick layer of mortar (more than ½") that is used for leveling.
- Apply thick layer of mortar ¾" (10 mm) to 1¼" (32 mm) to subfloor
- Set in mortar in 2 ways (stones 1½" (38 mm) to 2 ½" (64 mm))
  - Allowed to become semi-wet then set
  - Allowed to dry completely and then stone is set with a thin layer of dry-set mortar on top of the first
- Can be bonded directly to subfloor
- Can be separated from subfloor with a cleavage membrane usually a steel reinforcing mesh in the mortar bed

Grout
- Cementitious or other type material used for filling joints between tile and stone (Portland cement)
- Flexible material that allows for floor expansion (Latex)

Paste
- Water and cement

Construction Bonding Agents

Substances capable of holding materials together by surface attachment
Described as follows
- Physical (liquid adhesive, tape adhesive)
- Chemical type (silicate adhesive, resin adhesive)
- Materials bonded (paper adhesive)
- Conditions of use (hot-set adhesive)

TYPES

Bituminous binder
A class of black or dark-colored solid, semisolid or viscous cementitious substances, natural or manufactured, composed principally of high molecular weight hydrocarbons (asphalts, tars, pitches and asphaltites) used to cement loose materials together.

Casein glues
- Slow setting, permitting easier construction of difficult assemblies

Construction adhesive
- A high performance adhesive for multi-purpose in most interior and exterior construction projects
- Bonds all wood to wood assemblies
- Waterproof and weather proof
- Reduces Nail Pops
- Permanent bond

Contact Cements
- Useful for applying laminates and edge stripping to plywood.
- Not recommended for structural joints.

Epoxy
- Comes in two parts which you mix together -- resin and hardener -- with varying setting times.
- When fully cured, the provide a very tough, durable coating of high adhesive, cohesive, tensile and compression strength and are resistant to water, moisture and most chemicals.
- Most are not formulated for wood
- Used as a bonding agent to adhere new concrete to old surfaces; to rebond or weld structural units together; or as a matrix to be mixed with sand for patching, filling, grouting and general adhesive work.

High-Tech Adhesives
- Stronger than white glue, formulated to bond a variety of materials together including non-porous to non-porous, e.g., vitreous glass to glazed ceramic
- May be water-based (non-toxic) or solvent-based (toxic).

Wall panel adhesives
- Handy for applying decorative paneling or facing
- May require a few nails per panel to position panels while glue sets.

White Glue
- A general class of glues which as a rule are non-toxic, washable, and which dry clear
- Best used for bonding semi-porous and porous materials, e.g., ceramic to wood

JOINT SEALANTS

According to the American Concrete Pavement Association, there are three basic types of joint sealants: asphalt, silicone, and preformed sealants.

Asphalt joint sealants
- Hot-poured liquid sealants
- Generally the least expensive of the available sealants
- Lifespan from 5 to 8 years
- In most cases, traffic can resume on the pavement once the sealant has cooled.

Silicone sealants
- Cold-applied
- Highly flexible for transverse contraction and expansion joints, longitudinal, center line, and shoulder joints
- Last longer, from 10 to 15 years than asphalt

Preformed joint sealants (compression seals)
- Most expensive joint sealants
- Last up to 20 years
- No curing time necessary

Fuel resistant sealants
- More specialized type of sealant
- Made with silicone or coal tar
- Exhibit no physical or chemical change when exposed to fuels
- Commonly used in apron areas in airports, and even roadway bridge applications

Construction Equipment

Equipment may be self-propelled or attached to and operated off the hydraulic systems of equipment such as skid-steers, backhoes, and loaders.

Factors that affect the type of equipment used include:
- Type of soil (Most important)
- Confinement
- Trench depth and width
- Cost

EQUIPMENT TYPES

Rammers
- Deliver high impact force (high amplitude)
- Excellent choice for cohesive and semi-cohesive soils.
- Frequency range is 500 to 750 blows per minute.
- Inclined at a forward angle to allow forward travel as the machine jumps.
- Covers three types of compaction: impact, vibration and kneading.

Vibratory Plates
- Low amplitude and high frequency
- Designed to compact granular soils and asphalt.
- Drives weights at a high speed to develop compaction force.
- The heavier the plate, the more compaction force
- Frequency range is usually 2500 vpm to 6000 vpm.
- Plates used for asphalt have a water tank and sprinkler system to prevent asphalt from sticking to the bottom of the base plate.

Reversible Vibratory Plates
- Have two eccentric weights that allow smooth transition for forward or reverse travel, plus increased compaction force as the result of dual weights.
- Ideal for semi-cohesive soils due to their weight and force
- May be stopped and the machine will maintain its force for "spot" compaction.

Rollers
- Available as walk-behind or ride-ons
- Available as smooth drum, padded drum, and rubber-tired models
- Further divided into static and vibratory sub-categories

Smooth-drum
- Ideal for both soil and asphalt
- Dual steel drums are mounted on a rigid frame
- Frequency is around 4000 vpm and amplitudes range from .018 to .020.
- Vibration is provided by eccentric shafts placed in the drums or mounted on the frame.

Padded rollers (trench rollers)
- Effective in trenches and excavations
- Feature hydraulic or hydrostatic steering and operation.
- Built to withstand the rigors of confined compaction
- Either skid-steer or equipped with articulated steering
- Provide high impact force and high amplitude (for rollers) that are appropriate for cohesive soils.
- Drum pads provide a kneading action on soil.

Rubber-tire
- Usually equipped with 7 to 11 pneumatic tires with the front and rear tires overlapping
- Compaction force is altered by the addition or removal of weight added as ballast in the form of water or sand.
- The compaction effort is pressure and kneading, primarily with asphalt finish rolling.
- Tire pressures on some machines can be decreased while rolling to adjust ground contact pressure for different job conditions.

SOIL TYPE

The desired level of compaction is best achieved by matching the soil type with its proper compaction method. Other factors must be considered as well, such as compaction specs and job site conditions.

Sheep's foot roller
- Best for a colloidal soil condition
- Used exclusively with cohesive soils to allow for deep compaction of the materials

Plate compactors
- Best suited for aggregate products

Walk-behind tampers
- For small trench work

Double-drum vibrating roller
- Appropriate for asphalt work
- Require a machine with a high impact force to ram the soil and force the air out, arranging the particles.

Rammer/pad-foot vibratory roller
- Best used on cohesive soils if higher production is needed.

Vibratory plates (forward travel)
- Best choice for granular soils
- Allows the particles to fall freely of their own weight

EQUIPMENT APPLICATION

Granular Soils
- Vibratory Plates   Best Application

Sand and Clay
- Reversible Plates   Best Application
- Vibratory Rollers   Best Application

Cohesive Clay
- Rammers   Best Application
- Reversible Plates   Best Application

Asphalt
- Vibratory Plates   Best Application
- Vibratory Rollers   Best Application

EQUIPMENT

Chain Trencher — A self-propelled machine with blades attached to a continuous chain, used to excavate trenches.

Backhoe — An excavator in which a shovel mounted on the rear of a tractor, hydraulically operated to dig trenches or pits in soil.

Bobcat — A skid-steer loader and compact excavator can work simultaneously for optimal productivity on a job site, whereas a tractor/loader/backhoe can only do one task at a time — load or excavate.

Bulldozer — A heavy, driver-operated machine for clearing and grading land, usually having continuous treads and a broad hydraulic blade in front

Box scraper — An attachment that is used to remove materials, store it, transport to another location and then re-spread and compacts it.

Compact excavator — Also called "mini" excavators
Generally include those with operating weights of 14,000 lbs. or less and dig depths of 14' or less. Can slew 360º

Irrigation shovel — The same general design as a round point shovel, but it has a straighter shank Used for planting holes or ditches where a vertical side is desired.

Tract dozer — An excavation machine that moves on tracks to assist movement on soft or rugged terrain

Tractor/loader/backhoe (TLB) — Main competitor of the compact excavator
Limited to a maximum of 180º workgroup movement
Fold-down stabilizers often restrict its access to confined areas

Trencher — A variety of powered machines designed to dig trenches. Some trenchers are capable of multiple tasks in addition to digging the trench, such as laying drainage pipe and backfilling the trench.

Turf tires — Tires which are designed to be used on golf course and other expensive grass
Wheel Trencher — Trench digging machine that has a large, engine driven wheel with bucket shaped blades around it. Soil is removed from the trench by buckets, when the wheel turns, placing it on the sides of the trench.

Decks

Decks are a special feature of many new houses and a useful add-on to others.

CHARACTERISTICS

- Low maintenance materials
- Weather resistant
- Durable
- Slip-resistance
- Outdoor living space
- Good foundation
- Stable structure

DESIGN

The typical deck is elevated, set on a post and beam construction frame with a railing. Stairs are optional but usually desired. Dress-up features include the addition of benches, planters, arbors, lattice skirts and privacy lattice screening.
- Should be consistent with the general lines of the house
- Should be positioned to function as part of the total structure
- Orientation for sun exposure and shade is particularly important in the deck's location

Posts
The vertical structural element that rests on the footing and supports the beam
- Consist of 4 x 4 lumber
- Pressure preservative treated for ground contact
- Require footing holes at points.
- Use concrete or gravel bases of 4"minimum thickness below the frost line over compacted soil in footing holes.
- Measure length of post to the deck level from the concrete or gravel base
- Footings for naturally durable wood posts extend 6" above grade.

Beams
- Beams typically measure 4 x 6 and are usually made by nailing two 2 x 6 pieces back to back.
- Major load-carrying member
- Wood member should be sized according to wood span tables.

- **Beam Size** | **Max. Span Allowed when Laid on Edge**
  - 4x4 or two 2x4s — 4 ft (1m)
  - 4x6 or two 2x6s — 6 ft (1.5m)
  - 4x8 or two 2x8s — 8 ft (2m)
  - 4x10 or two 2x10s — 10 ft (2.5m)
  - 4x12 or two 6x10s — 12 ft (3m)
  - 6x10 or two 2x10s — 12 ft (3m)
  - 6x12 or two 2x12s — 14 ft (3.5m)

Joist

Horizontal framing members that support decking; a system of sub-deck structural elements located directly beneath the deck boards

- Commonly uses 2 x 6 or 2 x 8 lumber
- Commonly 16" or 24" for joist

Decking

- Face decking boards are 2 x 2, 2 x 4, or 2 x 6.
- Can be laid flat or positioned on edge
- Position the board so its end rings curve up. (bark side up)
- Normally 2" x 4" or 2" x 6" lumber
- Can nail decking pieces in contact or spaced no farther apart than a nail diameter where pressure preservative treated lumber or unseasoned naturally durable lumber species are used
- Can lay kiln dried decking with a maximum spacing of ¼"
- Must use good quality hot-dipped galvanized, aluminum or stainless steel decking nails
- Drive two 16d nails at slight angles to each other at each joist position,
- Use three nails for butt joints in 2" x 6" decking

Railings

- Must be securely anchored to the deck, preferably including an extension of the posts.
- Limit openings in the railing to 6", or as the code requires.
- Must be designed and constructed to withstand a concentrated load of 200 pounds applied at any point and any direction.
- Must design intermediate rails, balusters and panel fillers to withstand a horizontally applied load of 50 pounds on a one-square-foot area
- Must design the top of a guardrail at least 36" from the floor
- Must not allow the spacing in the guardrail ornamental pattern, balustrade or pickets to be more than a 4" diameter sphere
- Three categories:
  - Decorative Grade (for installation less than 30" off the ground)
  - Residential Grade (for installation more than 30" off the ground)
  - Commercial Grade (a railing height equal to or greater than 42" high)

FASTNERS FOR DECKS

Wood members can be joined together using nails, screws, bolts or lag screws. Metal nailing straps, joist hangers, post anchors and other special hardware pieces make joining members easier and more accurate. All fasteners and hardware must be **galvanized (zinc applied)** or otherwise **non-rusting** to prevent staining of the wood.

Nails
- Should penetrate the thicker back piece by twice the thickness of the thinner piece, but no more than 1½" (38mm)
- Use 3" (10d) nails to fasten decking with a nominal thickness of 2" (51mm) and 2½" (64mm), (8d) nails on decking with nominal thickness of 1¼" (32mm).
- Deck boards 2" (51mm) wide need one nail per joist while 4" (102mm) and wider decking requires two per joist.
- To prevent wood from splitting, use thin shanked nails with blunt points.

Note: Always nail through thinner members into thicker stock.

Screws
- Should penetrate the receiving member by at least the thickness of the thinner member, but never less than 1" (25mm)
- Penetration of 1½" (38mm) is required for structural components.
- Pilot holes for screws should be the diameter of the solid portion of the screw between the threads.

Carriage bolts
- Require washers under their nuts
- Pilot holes for bolts should be the same diameter as the bolt shank.

Lag screws
- Should be installed with a washer
- Pilot holes for lag screws should be the diameter of the solid portion of the screw between the threads.
- Requires flat washers at both their head and nut ends to keep from crushing the wood when tightened.

Blind Fastening Systems
- Create a fastener-free deck surface
- Employ metal clips and/or joist top brackets that fasten the sides or bottom of the deck board to the joists so that no fasteners are visible.

FINISHES

Pressure-treated and naturally durable wood are resistant to decay and insects.
- Use a good water-repellent stain or paint finish to protect against checking and to maintain the attractiveness of the deck
- Recommend that an application of a clear water repellent preservative be applied immediately upon completion of the deck for both pressure treated and naturally durable lumber.

CONCEPTS.

Anchor Plate/Tie Plate/Tie Bars — A plate, usually metal, on the face of a wall over which the ends of structural iron reinforcements (tie bars) are bolted or pegged
Sometimes referred to as tie plates, they are often quite decorative
Baluster (Spindle) — One of a series of vertical supports used between posts of a railing
Cap Rail — The top horizontal piece of a railing, usually placed to give it a finished appearance.
Composite Decking — Deck boards manufactured from wood fiber and plastic to form a profile which requires less maintenance and generally has a longer lifespan than natural wood.
Fascia (Skirt) — The boards used to cover rim joists and end joists.
Fasteners — Generic term for nails, bolts, screws and other connecting devices
Flashing — The system used to seal membrane edgings at walls, expansion joints, drains, gravel stops and other places where the membrane, cap or counter flashing shields the upper edges of the base flashing.
Flatness — Flatness is a measure of a cut length steel sheet's ability to conform to a flat horizontal surface. Maximum deviation from that surface is the degree to which the sheet is out of flat. Flatness is often expressed quantitatively in either Steepness or I-Units.
Footing — The below-ground support of a deck's post, usually made from concrete.
Furring — The method of finishing the interior face of masonry wall to provide space for insulation, to prevent moisture transmittance, or to provide a smooth or plane surface for finishing
Hanger — Any of a class of hardware used in supporting or connecting members of similar or different materials as, for instance, a stirrup strap or beam hanger for supporting the end of a beam or joist at a concrete foundation wall.
May also be referred to as a connector
Joist Hanger — A pre-manufactured metal piece typically attached to a ledger or beam to support a joist. Joist hangers should be galvanized.
Ledger — A length of board, that is horizontally attached to the side of a house and holds up one edge of a deck.
Nail-on/Tie Plate — Light-gauge steel truss connector plates with or without pre-punched holes, through which nails are driven by hand or pneumatic means into the lumber
On Center — A method of measuring distance between two structural members, such as joists where you measure from the center of one member to the center of the other
Joists spaced 16" on center are actually 14½"" apart.
Pier Block — A masonry post
Often serve as above-grade footings for posts and often are made of pre-cast concrete.
Post Anchor — A metal piece attached to or imbedded in the footing that attaches the post to the footing and keeps the post from being exposed to moisture in the ground.
Post Cap — A small piece of material (often wood) attached to the top of the post to cover the post's wood grain and protect the post from the weather.
Can be made of many materials including metal, injection-molded plastics, decorative glass tops for round and square posts
Shade Structure — A structure built above decks, usually of posts and lattice, to provide a shaded area on the deck.
Span — The distance between supports
Sub-Structure — Construction located below and supports the deck boards and railing system
Components include joists and hangers, ledgers, rim joists, beams, posts, anchors and footers.

Fasteners

Fasteners are an essential part of any construction project. There are many different types and sizes to fit a wide range of applications.

NAILS

Corrosion-resistant
- Hot-dipped galvanized
  - Most widely used and economical
  - Recommended for outdoor applications
  - For use with treated wood
- Aluminum
- Stainless steel nails

Size
- Generally are 1" to 6" in length, usually getting thicker as they get longer.

Points
- Vary
- Four-sided diamond point most common

Heads
- Vary
- Smaller heads
  - Can be driven in
  - Can be painted over
- Corrugated heads
  - Large framing nails
  - Reduce the danger of a hammer slipping

Coatings and Deformations
- Strengthens nails
  - Adhesive coating creates a stronger bond. The adhesive heats up as the nail is driven.
  - As it cools, the bond solidifies.
  - Deformations such as rings, spirals or barbs drive into wood fibers to hold fast.
- Difficult to remove
- Will damage the wood when taken out.
- Nails with no coating are referred to as bright.

NAIL TYPE/DESCRIPTION/USE

Box
- Fastening when smaller stock is a concern
- Short, thin shape (smaller than common nails)
- Has a blunt tip that won't split wood easily

Brad

- Attaching molding to walls or furniture
- Smaller version of the finishing nail.
- Up to about 1" long

Casing

- Attaching case molding or rough trim where strength and concealment are required
- Similar to finishing nail, but thicker and heavier
- Has a small head like a finishing nail

Common

- Performing construction framing and other rough work
- Thick, heavy-duty, general-purpose nail
- Has a large, flat head

Cut Flooring

- Nailing flooring through edges without splitting the wood
- Has a rectangular body
- Has a blunt tip that won't split wood easily

Finishing

- Fastening trim and cabinets when nailheads should not show
- Small nail with cupped head
- Can be countersunk with a nailset, then filled over

Gutter Spikes

- Securing guttering
- Long (7-8") galvanized nail

Masonry or Concrete

- Securing materials such as wood to brick or concrete
- Made of thick, hardened steel with grooved or fluted shank
- Shank can be round, flat or square

Sinker

- Framing
- Thick-bodied nail with low-profile head
- Sometimes called a cooler nail

Spiral

- Securing flooring for tight, squeak-free joining
- Spiral shank nail that somewhat resembles a screw
- Tends to turn in like a screw as it's driven

Spike

- Performing heavy framing work or securing landscape timbers
- Large nails over 6" long
- Has either smooth or spiral shank

Rivet
- A short iron or soft steel rod with a head at one end
- Heated and put into a proper hole
- Other end is hammered down until a suitable head is formed

SCREWS

For fastening, screws are stronger than nails. They can be removed with less damage to the material (especially wood) than nails.

Size
- Range from ¼" to 6" long.
- Gauge is the diameter of the screw shaft (not including threads), rated by numbers 2-24. A larger gauge number indicates a larger screw.
- The longer a screw is, the harder it is to turn with a screwdriver.
- Consider a lag screw when you need something over 4" in length. Lag screws are turned with a wrench.

Material and Finish
Chrome, brass, brass plated, stainless steel, galvanized
- Galvanized (plated with zinc for rust-resistance) is recommended where wood will be attached to metal
- Exterior screws such as deck screws can react to certain types of wood. Specially treated screws are available for specific applications such as pine, cedar, birch or oak.
- Stainless steel can also react to the tannins in certain woods (oak for example)
- Bluing is a finishing (actually black in color) that prevents rust

Slot Type
- **Slotted**
  - Conventional single-groove screwhead, applied with a flathead screwdriver.
- **Phillips**
  - Cross-slotted screwheads with U or V-Shaped slots of uniform width
  - Driven with a Phillips screwdriver
  - Used in woodworking and drywall installation.
- **Torx™ or Robertson**
  - Require special drivers and are commonly used in electronics, metal or automotive applications.

Head Type
- **Oval**
  - Lower portion is countersunk and the top is rounded.
  - Easier to remove
- **Round**
  - Used where the fastened piece is too thin to permit countersinking
  - Used on parts that may require a washer.

- **Flat**
  - Used in applications where the head needs to be flush with the surface.
  - Slotted and Phillips

Other Styles
- **Self-tapping**
  - Cut and form a thread in the material
  - Used in fastening to thin sheet metal work
- **Self-drilling**
  - Have points that are designed and shaped like the tips of drill bits.
- **Fine-thread**
  - Works best for hardwoods.
- **Coarse-thread**
  - Intended for soft woods

Types
Most masonry anchors work in one of two ways--by expanding against the sides of the hole and gripping the concrete or by friction against the sides of the hole
- **Anchor bolts**
  - Long, usually L-shaped, bolt embedded in concrete or another strong material
  - Used to fasten to a foundation or other support
- **Expansion sleeves**
  - Used in concrete, masonry, grout-filled block and hollow block
  - May be made of lead (Not. recommended where lead is considered dangerous)
- **Fiber plug**
  - Jute fiber screw style anchor designed for use in concrete, block, brick, stone, and plaster
  - Designed for use with wood, sheet metal and lag screws
- **Carriage Bolt**
  - Smooth, round head bolt used in wood
  - Small square section under the head keeps the bolt from spinning while the nut is tightened on the other side
- **Cavity Wall Ties**
  - Metal ties or bonding units used to tie together the wythes on a cavity wall.
- **Deck**
  - Fastening in outdoor applications where strength and resistance to elements is essential
  - Similar is design to drywall screws but larger
  - Galvanized or specially treated for outdoor use
- **Dowel**
  - Fastening end-to-end wood joints
  - Threaded on both ends
- **Eye Bolt**
  - Has a loop or eye at one end in place of the customary flat head
  - Used in conjunction with a hillside washer for tensioning cable braces
- **Gutter**
  - Securing guttering
  - Long (7-8") treated screw

- **J-bolt**
  - Angled rod, usually steel, embedded in a concrete footing, or anchor, and threaded at the exposed top end for attachment to a freestanding sign
- **Lag**
  - Fastening where maximum holding power is needed
  - Pointed bolts
  - Come in varying diameters;
  - ⅜" is the most popular
  - Available in ¼", 5/16", and ½"
  - Made to be tightened with a wrench
  - Also called lag bolt
- **Machine Bolt**
  - Configured with a hex head and nut and a blunt end
  - Meant to hold two pieces (usually the support structure) by pinning them together, the threads hold only the nut and don't screw into the wood itself.
- **Nail drive anchors**
  - These anchors when driven in expand inside the hole for a secure grip.
  - Drill hole the same size as the anchor
  - Non-removable
- **Sheet Metal**
  - Attaching metal components
  - Short, thick screw
  - Usually zinc-plated, but can be stainless steel or aluminum
  - Heads can be Phillips or regular slotted
  - Head types can be oval, flat, round, or hex
  - Threaded all the way down the shank
- **Snap Tie**
  - Concrete form tie, which is factory made and holds the concrete forms in place at a certain distance.
  - The tie can be broken off after the concrete is poured and set and the forms are stripped, so that only a small area must be patched.
- **Through bolts**
  - Threaded rod that runs down through the entire wall system
  - Range in diameter from ½" to 1½"
- **Toggle Bolt**
  - A bolt with a separate toggle end that can be flattened to fit through a pre-drilled hole and that springs outward to provide securement when the bolt is tightened
  - Used in block, wallboard and other hollow base materials.
- **Wood**
  - Securing wood to wood
  - Threaded ¾ of the length of the screw
  - May be made from stainless steel, zinc chrome, or brass
  - Phillips or slotted head
  - Head types can be flat oval or round
  - Work best with a pre-drilled pilot hole

BRACKETS

Joist Hangers
Metal fasteners that attach joists to ledger board

Post Anchors
Metal brackets that attach the post to piers

Post cap
A decorative top that can be added to a railing post

Anchors
- Z anchor   L with dowel
- Z strap   U strap
- 'L' Strap   L anchor
- Split Strap   Split Anchor

SOLDER

An alloy of tin and lead with a comparatively low melting point used to join less fusible metals. Typical solder contains 60% tin and 40% lead - increasing the proportion of lead results in a softer solder with a lower melting point, while decreasing the proportion of lead results in a harder solder with a higher melting point.
- A good solder joint will be smooth and shiny.
- If the joint is dull and crinkly, the wire probably moved during soldering.
- If you have taken too long it will have solder spikes.

Finishes

With outdoor finished wood, the areas that deteriorate the fastest are those exposed to the greatest amount of sun and rain, usually on the south and west sides of a building.   Under normal conditions, the finish deteriorates first by soiling or accumulating slight chalk (as with a paint) or erodes away (as with semitransparent penetrating stain.)

VOC

Volatile organic compound is defined in federal rules as a chemical that participates in forming ozone and is subject to heavy environmental compliance regulation. The largest sources of reactive VOC emissions are transportation sources and industrial processes. Miscellaneous sources, primarily forest wildfires and non-industrial consumption of organic solvents, also contribute significantly to total VOC emissions.

By definition, a product is considered low-VOC if it contains less than 150 g/l

CLASSIFICATIONS

Exterior
- Used with exterior projects

Interior
- Used on interior projects
- Usually water soluble

Water-soluble
- Often marketed as varnish, polyurethane, lacquer, latex, acrylic or polyvinyl paints
- Always identifiable by some mention of water clean-up on the can
- Much less resistant to heat, solvent, acid, and alkali damage
- Has binder of vinyl chloride or acrylic resins

Oil base
- Called alkyd paints
- Have binders that dissolved in synthetic alkyd resin
- Durable and scrubbable

GLOSSES

Gloss
- Creates a shiny appearance
- Has the most sheen
- Usually washable
- Tend to show surface defects

Semigloss
- Creates a slightly shiny appearance
- Has a less sheen than gloss
- Usually washable
- Tend to show surface defects

Satin
- Has a dull luster
- Some washability

TYPES

Stain
- Clear, or water or solvent-based finish with added pigment
- Used on wood

Semi-transparent stains
- Contain pigments that partially block the effects of UV light
- Longevity generally better than varnish
- Upkeep is also less costly and simpler
- Good choice where some limited grain visibility is required
- Less costly than varnish

Opaque stains
- Last well better than their semi-transparent cousins
- Requires repainting every 5-7 years
- Often pigmented urethane tung oil varnishes

Epoxies
- Resists corrosion, chemicals, and abrasions
- Durable finish for concrete, metals and wood

Varnish
- The resins used today are synthetic alkyds, phenolics, and polyurethanes.
- One of the most protective and durable of all finishes

Polyurethane
- Technically a varnish made with polyurethane resins.
- More protective and durable than other types of varnish

Spar varnish
- Uses more oil and less resin
- Results in softer and more flexible varnish
- Best for outdoor use because it flexes better with outdoor wood movement

Urethanes
- Resist abrasion, grease, alcohol, water, and fuels
- Durable finish for wood floors and antigraffiti coating

Shellac
- Only natural resin still widely used to make a finish
- May not be as water-resistant as varnish or lacquer but is quite resistant.
- Breaks down slowly
- Varies in color between orange (amber) and clear
- Fast drying property is a real advantage for reducing dust problems

Lacquer
- Primary finish used in factories and professional finishers and refinishers
- Dries very fast, reducing dust problems
- Easy to apply with a spray gun
- Solvent fumes left by spraying lacquer are bad for your health.
- Can purchase in aerosol spray cans for finishing small projects

Paint

- Used as a coating to protect or decorate a surface (especially a mixture of pigment suspended in a liquid); dries to form a hard coating
- Provide the best possible finish in terms of longevity
- Average recoat interval for full sun applications averages 10 years
- Moderate cost finish overall

Enamels

- Made with a varnish or resin base
- Not true paint

FOAM INSULATION

Spray foam insulation is a two-part liquid containing a polymer (such as polyurethane or modified urethane) and a foaming agent.

- Sprayed through a nozzle into wall, ceiling, and floor cavities
- Expands into a solid cellular plastic with millions of tiny air-filled cells that fill every nook and cranny as it is applied
- Should be applied by a professional using special equipment to meter, mix, and spray into place
- Commonly used for retrofits, irregularly shaped areas and around obstructions
- Forms both insulation and an air barrier because it eliminates the steps for air-tightness detailing (such as caulking, applying house-wrap and vapor barrier, and taping joints).

OUTDOOR SIGNS

Use sign enamel with primer and block out over a carefully cleaned MDO substrate. MDO (medium density overlay) is the only suitable substrate for a paint-lettered sign that is intended to last more than a few months. It is the substrate governments stipulate for traffic signs and professional sign shops require for guaranteed wood signs.

Irrigation Systems

The main objective of an irrigation system is to supply adequate and timely water to plants. There are three basic types.

TYPES

Sprinklers

Commonly used for turf applications

- **Rotating Sprinklers**
  - Used to irrigate large areas (golf course)
  - Single or multiple nozzles, gears, cam or impact driven, spacing from 35" to 115"operating pressures from 40 to 100 psi
  - Flow rates from 6 to 65 gpm with average application rates varying between 0.25 and 1.0 inch/hour.

- **Fixed Spray Sprinklers**
  - Used to water small turf areas (residential landscape)
  - Can have full, part circle or rectangular patterns, with radiuses from 4' to 22' several angles of spray trajectory
  - Application rates ranging from less than 1 to over 2 inches per hour
  - Should be operated at low pressures 15 to 50 psi.
- **Pop-up systems**
  - Typically have the poorest uniformities
  - Not effective on many landscapes with slopes, mounds, compact or heavy soils.
- **Drip and Micro-Sprinklers**
  - Cross between spray nozzles and drip irrigation
  - Have low flow rates, low application rates, small radiuses
  - Operate with low pressures.
  - Well suited for small ornamental plantings and single trees or shrubs
  - Require filtered and pressure regulated water.

Drip

Drip or micro irrigation applies water to the soil at point locations at low controlled flow rates. All drip irrigation systems should include a filter and pressure regulator.

- **Drip Tubing**
  - Used to irrigate plantings in berms, isolated areas, and separate planter boxes
  - Emits water at equally spaced points (6" to 60") along a tube
  - Bi-Wall drip irrigation tubing has drip holes regularly spaced.
  - Porous drip irrigation tubing allows water to seep out along the entire length of the tube.
  - Can either be laid on top of the soil or buried in the soil
- **Bubblers**
  - Similar to drip emitters except that they have a much higher flow rate
  - Flood a small area and the water continues to infiltrate into the soil after the bubbler has been shutoff.
  - Applicable in areas where small basins can be constructed to contain the water and where the soil is surface is level.

Surface or Flood Irrigation

In surface irrigation the soil is the distributing and infiltration system can be used in a few horticulture situations

- Generally applies deeper irrigation
- Requires higher flow rates for a shorter period of time than sprinkler or trickle. Limited by the slope of the area

BASIC COMPONENTS

- Water source (municipal, effluent, well, etc.)
- Meter (may be required by water supplier)
- Backflow prevention and vacuum breaker device protect water supply. This is required by law and is also a good safety feature.
- Valves (manual or automatic) and wire.
- Pressure regulator (drip irrigation).

- Filtration system (drip irrigation).
- Controller and related hardware if using automatic valves. Most automatic valves are electric and require wires connecting the controller and valves.
- Distribution pipe and pipe fittings.
- Sprinklers, drip emitters, drip tubing or bubblers.

SPRINKLER PARTS

Anti-drain valve/check valve — A valve located under a sprinkler head to hold water in the system so it minimizes drainage from the lower elevation sprinkler heads.

Automatic controller — A mechanical or solid state timer, capable of operating valve stations to set the days and length of time of a water application

Backflow prevention device (double-check device) — A safety device used to prevent pollution or contamination of the water supply due to the reverse flow of water from the irrigation system
- Local code will specify the type.

Electric valve — Automatic valve usually controlled by 24 to 30 volt (AC) current.

Electric Zone Valves — Allows water to go to individual areas of property, which is referred to as zones. When one zone valve closes, another valve opens so that only one zone is irrigated at a time. The valves are located out in the field in fiberglass control boxes under the ground.

Emitter — Drip irrigation fittings that deliver water slowly from the system to the soil.

Fittings — Array of coupling and closure devices that include connectors, tees, elbows, goof plugs and end caps
- May be of several types including compression, barbed and locking

Goof plugs — Insertable caps to plug holes in mainline and microtubes where drip devices have been removed or aren't needed

Inlet — A narrow opening or valve through which a substance such as water, enters the a pump or other device

Lateral line — The water delivery pipeline that supplies water to the emitters or sprinklers from the valve

Main line — The pressurized pipeline that delivers water from the water source to the valve or outlet

Overhead sprinkler irrigation systems — Those with high flow rates (pop-ups, impulse sprinklers, rotors, etc)

Rain sensing device — A system which automatically shuts off the irrigation system when it rains

Sleeve — Tubing that slips over another.
- Hollow cylinder which allows another commodity to pass through

Soil moisture sensing device — A device that measures the amount of water in the soil

Sprinkler head — A device which sprays water through a nozzle

Valve — A device used to control the flow of water in the irrigation system.

Water Pressure Regulator (water pressure reducing valve) — Device that automatically reduces the high incoming water pressure from the city mains to a lower, more functional water pressure suitable for the home and "regulates" or maintains a set water pressure in the home - usually 50 psi

PIPES

There are 4 different types of NFS (National Safety Foundation) listed pipe that can be used in a system: Copper, PVC, Poly, and Funny pipe. Flow is measured in GPM (gallons per minute), friction loss is measured in PSI (pounds per square inch), and velocity is measured in FPS (feet per second).

Pipes should be sized so that they allow water to flow through optimally.

Maximum** Flow Rates (Gallons per Minute)

Pipe Type	½"	¾"	1"	1¼"	1½"	2"	
SCHEDULE	40	4	8	13	22	30	50
SCHEDULE 80	3	6	11	20	26	46	
CLASS 200	NA	10	16	26	36	55	
TYPE L COPPER	5	7	12	19	26	48	
P.E. (DRIP)*	4gpm	8gpm	13gpm	NA	NA	NA	
	240gph	480gph	780 gph				

ELECTRICAL

AWG-UF
- Classification of the direct burial wire used for automatic sprinkler systems.
  - Example: #14-1 AWG-UF means a 14 gauge wire, single wire cable, designed for direct burial (no conduit) in the ground.
- Should be at least 18" deep for safety (in most areas this requirement is written into local law).

VAC (Volts Alternating Current)
- Most electric control valves operate on 24 VAC. However, most valves can be activated using direct current also.

MAXIMIZING WATER CONSERVATION AND EFFICENCY

- Group plants with similar watering needs together.
- Avoid odd shapes and narrow strips for turf areas.
- Prepare and amend the soil by tilling, aerating, and enriching the soil with compost or fertilizer
- Add mulch to all planting beds to help control weeds, retain moisture, provide nutrients and prevent runoff.
- Water early in the morning when temperatures and winds are low and humidity is high.
- During the summer, occasionally water 10 to 15% more than is usually required. The extra water carries the dissolved salts safely below the active root zone and prevents harmful salt accumulations.

GREYWATER RECLAMATION SYSTEM

- Used to convert building wastewater into usable irrigation water
- Typically employs mechanical filters to remove larger contaminants called "floaters" and organic biofilters often referred to as "constructed wetlands", which further decontaminate the water on site.

URBAN BEST MANAGEMENT PRACTICE

A voluntary irrigation practice designed to reduce water use and protect water quality. BMP is economical, practical and sustainable, and maintains a healthy, functional landscape without exceeding the water requirements of the landscape.

CONCEPTS

Application rate — The depth of water applied to a given area, usually measured in inches per hour.

Applied water — The portion of water supplied by the irrigation system to the landscape

Bernoulli Effect — Fluid pressure drops as fluid velocity increases

Flow Rate (Q) — Volume of water flowing past a given point (pipes and valves) per unit of time commonly used are gallons per minute (gal/min or gpm) and acre-inches per hour (ac-in/hr).

Hydrozone — A portion of the landscaped area having plants with similar water needs that are served by a valve or set of valves with the same schedule

- Example: Naturalized area planted with native vegetation that will not need supplemental irrigation once established is a non-irrigated hydrozone.

Landscape Zone — Means a portion of the landscaped area having plants with similar water needs, areas with similar microclimate (i.e., slope, exposure, wind, etc.) and soil conditions, and areas that will be similarly irrigated

Major pressure loss — Losses that occur in straight pipes and ducts

Minor pressure loss — Losses that occur in system components such as valves, bends, tees add head loss common termed as minor loss to the fluid flow system.

- The minor loss can be significant compared to the major loss. When a valve is closed or nearly closed the minor loss is infinite. For an open valve the minor loss may often be neglected (a full bore ball valve).

Operating pressure — The pressure at which a system of sprinklers is designed to operate, usually indicated at the base of a sprinkler.

Overspray — The water which is delivered beyond the landscaped area, wetting pavements, walks, structures, or other non-landscaped areas

Plant factor — A factor that when multiplied by reference evapotranspiration, estimates the amount of water used by plants.

Recreational area — Areas of active play or recreation such as sports fields, school yards, picnic grounds, or other areas with intense foot traffic

Recycled water/reclaimed water/treated sewage effluent water — Treated or recycled waste water of a quality suitable for nonpotable uses such as landscape irrigation; not intended for human consumption.

Reference evapotranspiration/ETo — A standard measurement of environmental parameters which affect the water use of plants

Run off — Water which is not absorbed by the soil or landscape to which it is applied and flows from the area

Static water pressure — The pipeline or municipal water supply pressure when water is not flowing

Station — An area served by one valve or by a set of valves that operate simultaneously.

Velocity (v) — Average speed at which water moves in the direction of flow. The velocity unit commonly used is feet per second (ft/sec or fps).

Voltage drop — The voltage that occurs across a solid-state device when its output is driving a load or the voltage that exists across each element of a series circuit.

- Magnitude of the voltage drop is dependent upon the circuit demand of the load

Lighting

Lighting systems are safe, economical, energy efficient and provide numerous benefits. Lighting can be used to accentuate architectural features, textures, landscaping, groundcover, and many other features at night.

GOALS

Residential

- Increase the curb appeal of your home
- Add value to your property
- Provide beautiful visual effects
- Accent special features
    - Example: Old oak tree
- Provide safety and security
    - Example: Definition to the sidewalk and steps so people won't stumble.
    - Light up landscape to deter intruders
- Encourage the use of a space at night
    - Example: playing or for cookouts
- Create different moods
    - Example: Lighting around the pool or patio can create that tropical feeling

Outdoor recreational area

- Provide a luminous environment that contributes to the contrast of the playing object (ball), the competitors, and the surrounding backgrounds.
- Provide uniform visibility to the players
- Minimize spill light, or light trespass

LIGHTING TYPES

High-Intensity Discharge (HID) Generic term that describes mercury vapor, metal halide, high-pressure sodium, and (informally) low pressure sodium light sources and luminaries
Most efficient lighting type
Can save up to 90% of lighting costs as compared to incandescent lights

- **Mercury vapor**
    - HID lamp in which most of the light is produced by radiation from mercury vapor
    - Light quality is blue-green and available in clear and phosphor-coated lamps
    - Used for street lighting and industrial applications (warehouses) where the color rendition of the light is not much of an issue.

- **Metal halide**
    - HID lamp in which most of the light is produced by radiation of metal halide and mercury vapors in the arc tube
    - Requires a protective outer bulb

  Clear – Facilitates optical control

  Phosphor-coated – Promotes better color qualities

  Diffuse- Used in low ceiling recessed downlight fixture

  Have better color rendition and higher lighting output (CRI between 60 – 90)
- **Low-pressure Sodium**
    - Very efficient but renders everything in tones of yellow and gray
    - Used in applications like highway lighting and security lights
- **High pressure sodium**
    - HID lamp whose light is produced by radiation from sodium vapor (and mercury)
    - Made of special ceramic material
    - Have efficacies from 80 – 140 lumens per watt
    - Used for outdoor lighting

Others lamps
- **Neon**
    - Can be manufactured in various shapes
    - Used for signs and specialty accent
    - Can produce a variety of colors

- **Cold-cathode**
    - Similar to neon but larger
    - Can be manufactured in longer lengths
    - Used for signs and specialty accent
    - Can produce a variety of colors and white
    - Has a higher efficacy

LOW VOLTAGE LIGHTING SYSTEMS

Low voltage lighting systems are frequently used in the landscape setting and consist of the following:
- A power pack (or transformer) supplies the electricity which plugs into a standard outlet and reduces the regular household current (120 volts) to a safe 12 volts.
    - Power packs have an automatic timer allowing lights to go on and off at preset times.
- A low voltage lamp is the source of light.
    - Lamps are available in a variety of brightness levels ranging from 4 watts up to 50 watts halogen.
- The low voltage cable transmits the electricity.

  Low voltage cable is a weather-resistant, self-sealing, insulated stranded copper wire that is available in 12-, 14- and 16-gauge sizes. The gauge required for your lighting is determined by the amount of watts required to operate your system:
    - 16-gauge cable can carry 150 watts
    - 14-gauge cable can carry 200 watts
    - 12-gauge cable can carry 300 watts

ELECTRICAL CONDUIT

- A properly installed metal conduit system is recognized by the National Electrical Code® (NEC®) as an equipment grounding conductor.
- The wall thickness and strength of steel make metal conduit the wiring method recognized as providing the most mechanical protection to the enclosed conductors.
- Normally 10' long

Types of steel conduit
- **RMC**
  - Has the thickest wall
  - Can be used indoors, outdoors, underground, and in both concealed and exposed applications
- **IMC**
  - Has a thinner wall
  - Weighs less than RMC
  - Can be used for the same applications as galvanized RMC
- **EMT**
  - Lightest-weight steel conduit manufactured
  - Easy to alter, reuse, or redirect EMT
  - Can be used in most exposed locations, except where severe physical damage is a possibility

PVC coatings
- May be used over bare or galvanized steel conduit or conduit that has a supplementary zinc coating
- May be used in severely corrosive locations and atmospheres

Steel tubing
- Similar to steel pipe, but available in a range of wall thickness and shapes, including round, square, and rectangular.
- Available in diameter sizes ranging from 5/8" to 2½"
- Easily welded or bolted
- Can be obtained in higher strengths than steel pipe

Sleeve
- Tubing that slips over another
- Hollow cylinder which allows another commodity to pass through

AC MOTORS

The most common and simple industrial motor is the three phase AC induction motor, sometimes known as the "squirrel cage" motor. It operates on AC current that flows in either direction (AC current). AC motors are designed and manufactured in four groups classified Design A, B, C, and D by NEMA. Each classification of motors has its own distinctive speed–torque relationship and inherent expectations regarding motor efficiency. The design "B" is the most common design. NEMA design B motors are general purpose single speed motors suited for applications that require normal starting and running torque such as fans, centrifugal pumps, and machine tools

Standard NEMA motor designs

NEMA Design	STARTING Torquecurrent	Starting Down Torque	Break-load Slip	Full Applications	Typical
A	Normal	High	High	Low	Mach., tools, fan
B	Normal	Normal	Normal	Normal	" " "
C	High	Normal	Low	Normal	Loaded compressor
D	Very high	Low	-----	High	High Punch Press

Horsepower (hp) categories
- **Small motors**
  - Fractional-horsepower motors with ratings from 1/20 to 1 hp
  - Motors with smaller ratings (sub-fractional or miniature)
- **Medium size motors**
  - In the range of 1 hp through 100 hp
  - Used in large quantities in industrial and consumer applications
- **Large motors**
  - 100 hp to 50,000 hp range

General types
- **Induction motor**
  - An alternating current motor in which the primary winding on one member (usually the stator) is connected to the power source and a secondary winding or a squirrel-cage secondary winding on the other member (usually the rotor) carries the induced current.
  - No physical electrical connection to the secondary winding
  - Current is induced
    - Example: Lumber saw
- **Synchronous motor**
  - Operates at a constant speed up to full load
  - The rotor speed is equal to the speed of the rotating magnetic field of the stator; there is no slip.
  - Often used where the exact speed of a motor must be maintained
    - Example: Timing such as time keeping, (clocks)

Default value
- A value stored in the system that is used when no other value is specified
- The default values will automatically reset when the system is reset. A reset occurs when the power is turned off and on, when the reset button is pushed

Universal motor
- Ac/dc motor that finds wide use in small electric appliances
- Operate at lower efficiency than either the ac or dc series motor
- Built in small sizes only
- Do not operate on polyphase ac power.

ASHRAE ENERGY STANDARDS

Society of Heating, Refrigerating and Air-Conditioning Engineers, Inc
Applies to:
- Interior spaces of buildings
- Exterior building features
- Exterior building grounds lighting provided through the building's electrical service

Exceptions:
- Emergency lighting that is automatically shut off during normal building operation
- Lighting within living units
- Lighting that is specifically designated as required by a health or life safety statute, ordinance, or regulation
- Decorative gas lighting systems

Exterior Lighting Control

Lighting for all exterior applications shall be controlled by a photosensor or by astronomical time switch that is capable of automatically turning off the exterior lighting when sufficient daylight is available or the lighting is not required.
- **Exceptions**
  - Lighting for covered vehicle entrances or exits, from buildings or parking structures, where required for safety, security or eye adaptation.

Exit Signs

Exit sign luminaires operating at greater than 20 watts shall have a minimum source efficacy of 35 lm/W

Exterior Building Grounds Lighting

All exterior building grounds luminaires that operate at greater than 100 watts shall contain lamps with a minimum efficacy of 60 lumens/watt or be controlled by a motion sensor.

Prescriptive Path

The exterior lighting power allowance is the sum of lighting power allowances for all applicable exterior applications permitted, other than building facades, provided the total installed exterior lighting power does not exceed the exterior lighting power allowance. See table below for Lighting Power Limits.

Lighting used for the following exterior applications is exempt when equipped with an independent control device.
- Specialized signal, directional, and marker lighting associated with transportation
- Lighting used to highlight features of public monuments and registered historic landmark structures or buildings
- Lighting that is integral to advertising signage

CONCEPTS

Accent Lighting — Used to accent or highlight a particular object
- Should be approximately 4 - 5 times the level of ambient light in the area to be effective accent lighting

Ambient Lighting — General lighting that usually lights up an entire space

Color Rendering Index (CRI) — A measure of a lamp's ability to render colors accurately. The scale ranges from 1 (low pressure sodium) to 100 (the sun). A CRI of 85 is considered to be very good.

Foot-Candle — The amount of light reaching a subject
- The commonly United States unit of measurement of lighting level (illumination) is the foot-candle (fc). The international unit of measurement of lighting level (Illumination) is the lux (lx). The relationship between the lux and the foot-candle is 1 fc = 10.76 lux.

Ground Clamps —Ground wires should not be merely wrapped around a ground rod. Ground clamps are used to attach a ground wire to a ground rod. The most common clamp is known as an acorn clamp. Must be rated for outdoor use.

Ground rod — A conducting connection by which an electric circuit or equipment is connected to the earth or to some conducting body of relatively large extent that serves in place of the earth
- National electrical code requires ground rod end to be below the surface unless protected from physical damage. No particular depth required just below the surface.
- The minimum length of a ground rod is 8'.
- Should be located close to the main breaker panel

Ground Wire — Large copper wire that connects the main breaker panel bus to the ground rod
- Typically, 6-gauge copper wire is sufficient. If the wire run is greater than 20', 4-gauge wire should be used. The ground wire should be protected from damage from lawnmowers and vehicles. It should be buried (min. 6") for protection.
- Metal conduit should not be used to carry a ground.

Lumen — A unit of measure used to describe the amount of light that a lamp (light bulb) produces or emits.

Luminaire — A complete lighting unit, consisting of a lamp or lamps together with the components required to distribute the light, position the lamps, and connect the lamps to a power supply.

Lumber

Lumber results when logs have been sawn, planed, and cut to length.

COMMON TERMS

Air dried lumber — Dried by being exposed to natural air rather than with the aid of heating devices
- Lumber that has been piled in yards or sheds for any length of time.

Board Feet — The most common measure used to describe log and lumber volume. A board foot is a board measuring 12" x 12" x "1 thick.

Common — Have obvious defects such as knots

Dressed lumber — Been finished or planed so it has a smooth finish.

Dressed sized lumber — The actual dimension of lumber after shrinking from its green higher moisture content dimensions and after being machined /planed smooth.

- Example: Standard 2" x 4" stud is actually 1 5/8ᵗ" x 3½"

Finish (lumber) — A term indicating the higher grades of lumber, sound, relatively free of blemishes

Green (unseasoned) — Freshly sawed lumber or lumber that has received no intentional drying

Glued-laminated structural timber (Glulam) — Large beams fabricated by bonding layers of specially selected lumber with strong, durable adhesives. End and edge jointing permit production of longer and wider structural wood members than are normally available.

- Used with structural wood panels for many types of heavy timber construction

Heavy Timber — A building code designation for a particular type of construction with good fire endurance

Kiln — Chamber or tunnel used for drying and conditioning lumber, veneer, and other wood products in which the environmental conditions can be varied and controlled.

LF: Lineal (running) foot — A measurement of the length of a board

Moisture Content (M.C.) — The weight of water contained in wood expressed as a percentage of the weight of the oven dry wood. The lower the percent, the less shrinking and warping in the lumber

Nominal Size

The rough-sawn size of a piece of lumber

Example: 2"x4" is the nominal size for a 1.4" x 3.25" board

Typical S2S Thicknesses (hardwoods):

Nominal	Actual
4/4 (1")	13/16"
5/4 (1-1/4")	1-1/16
6/4 (1-1/2")	1-5/16"
8/4 (2")	1-3/4"

Pitch pockets — Defects resulting from resin accumulations

Rough-sawn — Lumber that is either green or dried that has not been dressed.

S2S — A lumber-industry abbreviation for "surfaced on two sides". These boards are planed on both faces to final thickness after milling and drying.

S3S — An abbreviation for "surfaced on three sides". Here, boards get planed on both faces, and then straight-line ripped on one edge.

S4S — An abbreviation for "surfaced on four sides". These boards get planed on both faces, and then ripped on both edges to make them parallel. Usually produces "dimensional" lumber in standard sizes, such as 1 x 6, 2 x 4

Shrinkage — The contraction of wood fibers caused by drying below the fiber saturation point (usually around 25-27% M.C.)

Square Foot (SF) — A square unit of area measuring twelve inches on each of its four sides

Tensile Strength — The maximum load at which a specimen breaks under tension

Warping — Bending or twisting from a straight line. An improperly seasoned piece of lumber may warp when exposed to heat or moisture. Painting and water-repellent dips will minimize moisture absorption. Sealing all edges and back-priming also reduces the chances of warping in cabinet doors.

LUMBER GRADES

Lumber grades are determined by the number, location and size of defects in the board, not its strength. (The clearer the wood, the higher the grade)

Grades of hardwoods

Determined by characteristics such as knots, splits, and slope of the grain that affects the strength of the lumber. Grades are listed from highest to lowest.

Grade Name	Abbreviation	Minimum Board Size On One Face	% Usable Material
Firsts and Seconds	FAS	6" x 8'	83
Select	Sel	4" x 6'	83
#1 Common	#1 Com	3" x 4'	66
#2 Common	#2 Com	3" x 4'	50

There are grades below #2 Common, but they are typically not suitable for woodworking.

Grades of Softwoods

Softwoods are divided into two categories: dimensional lumber, with a grade based on strength, and appearance boards, which are typically used for woodworking projects. Grading of softwoods is overseen by a number of different agencies, so you will be more likely to find some variations in terminology. Grades listed here are from highest to lowest.

Grade	What It Means
C Select	Almost completely clear of defects. Widely used for interior trim and cabinets.
D Select	Fine appearance, similar to C Select. May have dime-sized knots
1 Common	Best material for high quality pine with a knotty look Knots will be tight (won't fall out and are generally small)
2 Common	Tight knots, but larger than found in 1 Common. Used for paneling, shelving general, woodworking projects
3 Common	Knots larger than in 2 Common. Well-suited for fences, boxes, and crates

Typical Lumber Grading Stamp

Lumber of the same species and size is designated and separated by grade. It is then identified by a stamp. There are five pieces of information included in every grade stamp:

- The identification number or name of the mill where the lumber is produced.
- The agency or association that certified the material.
- The species of wood
- The grade of the lumber
- The seasoning of the lumber, including the moisture content and method of drying

FRAMING

The structural wood and/or metal elements of most homes

Post and Beam — Any buildings that have upright posts supporting horizontal beams

Rough framing — The construction of the wooden structural framework of a building
- Includes the framing of the floors, wall, ceiling and roof joists

Timber framing — Means part or all of the home is constructed in a controlled environment before being delivered to the building site
- Specific type of post and beam construction in which a frame is created from solid wood timbers that are then connected by wooden joints
- Structural components remain exposed to the interior, allowing their geometry to function as an integral decorative element

Timber Post and Beam — Structures made of heavy timber, fastened with metal brackets

Light frame construction — Considered rough carpentry
- Concealed by finished walls and ceilings

Heavy timber construction

A type of combustible construction in which a degree of fire safety is attained by placing limitations on the sizes of wood structural members and on thickness and composition of wood floors and roofs and by the avoidance of concealed spaces under floors and roofs

Masonry/Stone Masonry

Masonry is the practice of building a structure made of stone or brick in which the materials are bound together by mortar. Common materials include clay, brick, concrete and various types of stones such as marble, granite, concrete block and limestone.

BENEFITS

- Strength
- Permanence
- Pest and weather resistant
- Fireproof.
- Energy efficient
- Requires low maintenance
- Increases resale value

WATERPROOFING MASONRY

- Mortar Joints
  - Concave and V type mortar joints are more weather resistant.
  - Well-tooled joints compact the mortar, filling voids and cracks
- Drainage cavity behind veneer wythe
- Flashing system at base of veneer

- Seals for the cavity at fenestrations (window, door, louver frames, etc.)
- Lateral tie system to anchor veneer to the structural back-up
- Vertical support system to support weight of veneer
- Provisions for expansion/contraction of the wall system
    - Movement Joints
    - Shrinkage and temperature cracks can develop without these joints, which allow passage of moisture to pass through the masonry.

TYPES OF WALL TIES

- **Unit ties**
    - Can be rectangular ties or "Z" ties
    - Fabricated from cold-drawn steel wire, stainless steel
    - Metal "Z" ties should only be used between wythes of solid masonry units in brick masonry cavity walls.
    - Rectangular ties can be used for all brick masonry cavity walls are therefore recommended instead.
- **Horizontal joint reinforcement**
    - Typically produced in 10' - 12' (3 to 4 m) lengths
    - Longitudinal wires are typically W1.7 [No. 9 gage, (0.148 in.) (3.8 mm)] or W2.8 [3/16 in. (4.8 mm)] diameter wire.
    - Cross wires should be spaced at a maximum of 16". (400 mm) on center horizontally and without drips
    - The total thickness of the wires should not exceed ½ the joint thickness.
- **Adjustable ties**
    - Typically have two-pieces consisting of a double eye and pintle configuration.
- **Truss design**
    - Prefabricated reinforcement for embedment in the horizontal mortar joints of masonry
    - Consists of two or more parallel and deformed longitudinal wires welded to a continuous diagonal cross wire
- **Corrosion**
  There are three types of materials used for corrosion protection of wall ties: galvanizing (zinc coatings), stainless steel and epoxy coatings

UNIT MASONRY ASSEMBLIES

- Usually used for the interior wythe of a cavity wall in combination with a brick masonry exterior
- May also be used as accent bands in the exterior brick wythe.
- Usually specify non load-bearing concrete masonry units for the interior wythe when the brick and block cavity wall is used as infill walls for concrete or steel frame structural systems if shear loads are not transmitted to that wythe.
- Consists of the following:
    - Concrete masonry units (CMUs)
    - Mortar and grout
    - Reinforcing steel
    - Masonry joint reinforcement
    - Ties and anchors

- o Embedded flashing
- o Miscellaneous masonry accessories

<u>Definitions</u>

Wythe: A continuous vertical section of a masonry wall, one unit in thickness.

Single wythe wall: A wall composed of a single unit of masonry in thickness (a one brick   or block thick wall).

Structural backing: the masonry or other system of structural members to whichmasonry veneer is tied. It is designed to withstand lateral loads (i.e. wind and earthquake loads).

Veneer: A non-loadbearing masonry facing attached to and supported by the structural backing.

Rainscreen wall: an exterior wall assembly that contains a drainage cavity between the structural backing and the cladding.

Cavity wall: A construction of masonry units laid up with a cavity between the wythes. The wythes are tied together with metal ties or bonding units and are relied on to act together in resisting lateral loads

ANCHORING PRODUCTS

Epoxy

A class of synthetic, thermosetting resins which produce tough, hard, chemical resistant coating and excellent adhesives
General uses include
- Crack sealing and port placement
- Bonding between existing and new concrete
- Structural crack injection
- Surface patching and spall repair
- Waterproof sealant
- Security sealant

Caulking — A term that refers to any elastic sealant used in construction
Epoxy sealer — A 2-component system that reacts when mixed to form a hard, durable sealer
Can be UV sensitive and are not heat resistant
Grout — A thin mortar used to fill cracks in masonry and tile.
Grout (Non-Shrink) — A cementitious material used to partially fill penetration pockets (pitch pans). A pourable sealer is used afterward.
- Ideal for grouting column bases, precast walls, panels, beams, pre-tensioned or post-tensioned pre-stressed member applications

Joint sealer — Caulking compound
Tends to be shiny, thick and look like plastic
Mastic — Heavy-consistency compound that may remain adhesive and pliable with age
- Is typically a waterproof compound applied to exterior walls and roof surfaces.

CLASSES OF JOINT FINISHES

Trowelled — Excess mortar is simply cut off (struck) with a trowel and finished with the trowel tooled
Special tool — Used to compress and shape the mortar in the joint.
- Only the concave, v-shaped, grapevine, and weathered are recommended for exterior use.

JOINTS

Joints are pre-planned cracks in concrete slabs created by forming, tooling, sawing, and placement.

Construction joints
- The surfaces where two successive placements of concrete meet
- Designed to permit movement and/or to transfer load in slabs
- Preinstalled dividers such as redwood strips, aluminum keyways, or other physical barriers

The following recommended practices should be observed:
- The maximum joint spacing should be 24 to 36 times the thickness of the slab. For example, in a 4" [100 mm] thick slab the joint spacing should be about 10' [3 m].
- Joint spacing be limited to a maximum of 15' [4.5 m].

- All panels should be square or nearly so. The length should not exceed 1.5 times the width. Avoid L-shaped panels.
- For contraction joints, the joint groove should have a minimum depth of ¼ the thickness of the slab, but not less than 1" [25 mm].

Contraction joints (also referred to as control joints)
Intended to create weakened planes in the concrete and regulate the location where cracks, resulting from dimensional changes, will occur.
Usually installed with a concrete saw after the concrete gets hard or a jointing tool while the concrete is still fresh

Head joint (Cross joint)
The vertical mortar joint between ends of masonry units

Isolation or expansion joints
Separates or isolates slabs from other parts of the structure, such as walls, footings, or columns; and driveways and patios from sidewalks, garage slabs, stairs, lightpoles and other points of restraint.

PAVERS
Primary considerations in selecting a unit paver system are cost, appearance, and the paver system's ability to endure expected traffic exposure and weather.

Unit
- **Brick pavers**
  - Light-traffic paving brick generally supports pedestrian and light vehicular traffic in applications such as patios, walkways, floors, plazas, and driveways
  - Heavy vehicular paving brick is used in pavements subjected to a high volume of heavy vehicles, which is defined as numerous passes of daily truck traffic
- **Concrete pavers** include small, "hand-size," solid units of high compressive strength
  - Made from concrete, available in a variety of sizes and shapes
  - Can be laid in many patterns and designs
- **Asphalt-block pavers** are units made from asphalt cement, crushed-stone aggregate, and inorganic dust or filler, which are compacted under hydraulic pressure. They are available in many shapes, sizes, thicknesses, colors, and finish textures.
- **Rough-stone pavers, (cobblestones)** are the oldest and perhaps most durable unit pavers in general use. They are split to size from granite, in roughly rectangular shapes, and may be tumbled after splitting to give them a worn appearance. These pavers are generally laid in mortar with medium to wide joints
- **Concrete masonry unit (CMU)**
  - A masonry unit made of Portland cement, water, and mineral aggregates, formed into a rectangular prism

Porous Paving
- Poured-in-place continuous surface:
  - Pervious concrete
  - Porous asphalt

- Unit pavers
  - Interlocking concrete pavers
  - Turf block
  - Brick
  - Natural stone
- Granular materials:
  - Crushed aggregate (gravel)

Applications
- Low traffic or pedestrian areas
- Overflow parking, "hybrid" lots
- Driveways, temporary parking areas
- Patios, plazas
- Emergency access or utility roads
- Storage or recharge beds under
- Parking lots

Metal Fabrication

Metal fabrication is the interpretation of technical drawings and layout of metal components, cutting and shaping of those components, through to assembly and welding or fastening to create the finished product.

Among the many fabricated items include cast iron and wrought iron fencing, home and garden accessories, indoor and outdoor furniture, fountains, driveway gates, cast iron urns, wrought iron furniture, iron and steel fence.

Angle iron
- A structural steel angle
- Used for lintels to support masonry over openings, such as doors, windows or fireplaces

Wrought iron
- Description of decorative ironwork that is made of any metal including wrought iron, steel, cast iron and aluminum
- Used to describe low carbon steel pipe

Outdoor Flooring

TYPES

Ceramic tile
- Made from clay or a mixture of organic materials and finished by kiln firing.
- Can be glazed or unglazed
- Glazed generally have a durable exterior coating that is more resistant to moisture

Cobblestone
- Naturally rounded stone larger than a pebble and smaller than a boulder used in paving a street or in construction

Flagstone
- Type of flat stone used for paving, roofing and building.

Granite
- Hard, dense stone for inside and outside surfaces

Sandstone
- Use when creating a large variety of things useful in a garden, kitchen, living room, walls, bathroom

Slate
- Hard varieties of slate are used in outdoor flooring and in areas of medium traffic.

Terrazzo
- Man-made stone that is frequently used in floors in high and medium traffic zones. Rustic terrazzo surfacing is excellent to reduce slip-and-fall accidents around pools, stairs, and other slippery surfaces.

Travertine
- Type of limestone that is often used outside as cladding and pavement

FINISHES

Polished
- A high gloss surface

Honed
- Smooth with squared edges and without a polished surface.

Tumbled
- Lightly tumbled to achieve rounded edges and a surface that is not as smooth as honed

Antique Tumbled
- Medium tumble edges and surface to achieve a slight rustic look

Cobbled or Distressed
- Heavily tumbled edges and surface to achieve an aged or ancient look

Brushed
- Acid washed and wire brushed for a smooth textured surface.

Flamed
- Blow torched for a rough textured surface.

DRAINAGE

Floor drain
- A drain designed to receive and convey run-off water or other liquid from building floors to the drainage system.

Retaining Walls

A retaining wall is designed to stabilize and control erosion of steeply sloped areas. In some cases, retaining walls are used in conjunction with terracing to provide a level area for recreational purposes. They should be designed to withstand the lateral pressures being exerted on them by the soil and the hydrostatic pressures from behind the wall.

CODES

In most states, retaining wall designs taller than about 4' must be designed by or approved by a qualified, licensed professional engineer. It is important to check with and adhere to local building codes prior to any construction, even when walls are shorter than 4'. Retaining walls are, and should always be viewed as load bearing members first, and aesthetic groundscapes second.

COMPONENTS

Materials
- May be built with concrete, construction timbers, railroad ties, stone, concrete or concrete blocks
- May be steel baskets filled with stones

Drainage
Provisions for drainage of water that normally accumulates include
- Continuous perforated drain lines at the lower portion of the wall and backfilling the areas with stone and gravel.
- Weep holes in the bottom of concrete retaining walls to allow the water to exit through the front of the wall.
- Grade soil at the base of the drainage system behind the wall to direct any water that accumulates to the weep holes

Anchors
Anchored retaining wall built with construction timbers or railroad ties to the hillside by using
- Tiebacks
- Deadmen tieback

Drain Zone
The zone immediately behind the retaining wall that is designed to free flow water from the retaining wall and its surround
Designed to relieve associated pressure buildup and to not be prone to clogging

Filter fabric
A cloth used to separate particles from their suspension in air or liquids.

Geosynthetics
Synthetic material or structure used as an integral part of a project, structure, or system. Within this category are subsurface drainage and water control materials such as geomembranes, geotextiles, and geocomposites

GRAVITY WALL

Relies on the weight and batter of the retaining wall to resist the loads imposed on the structure
A unit stack system composed of materials such as stack stone or keystone block.
Examples:

Crib Wall
- A type of retaining wall made from stacked concrete members that form vertical box columns and are filled with solid earth materials.

Gabions
Free-draining walls constructed by filling large baskets with broken stone. The baskets are made from galvanized steel mesh, woven strips, or plastic mesh. They can also be made from wickerwork, bamboo slats, nylon or polypropylene. A typical basket is rectangular with dimensions of about 50 cm by 15 cm.

Dry stack stone
- A wall of stones that is not held together by mortar
- Dry-wall construction requires greater precision in the way stones are stacked than does mortared-wall construction, since proper placement alone keeps the wall intact.

Batter/ Tilt-back
As applied to walls, the difference between the wall face alignment and vertical. Batter can be expressed in degrees or ratio of vertical to horizontal. A lean of the wall face towards the retained fill is considered a positive batter, while an outward lean is considered a negative batter. Batter is often built into a wall by off-setting or "setting back" successive courses of a wall by a specified amount

CANTILEVER WALL (STEM WALL)

- Has the greatest potential for height gain
- Composed of a vertical or inclined slab monolithic with a slab base
- Simple forms of cantilever wall utilize the weight of the earth or backfill on the heel. This weight is added to the concrete weight to provide resistance against active thrust.
- Usually cast in place and are used for moderate to high walls.

REVETMENT WALLS

- Large earth retaining systems that stabilize slopes and are often used as alternatives to an embankment fill slope
- May be constructed of fascines, wood, sandbags, gabions, sod, or masonry to protect a wall or bank of earth
- Wall inclinations are typically 70º to 90º with respect to the horizontal

SEGMENTAL RETAINING WALLS

Facing systems
- Usually consist of modular concrete blocks that interlock with each other and with the lateral restraining members.

Lateral tiebacks
- Usually geogrids that are buried in the stable area of the backfill. In addition to supporting the wall
- Stabilize the soil behind the wall which allows higher and steeper walls to be constructed.

BIOENGINEERING WALL

A reinforced embankment using geotextile materials, planting, stone, or concrete surfacing

LANDSCAPE RETAINING WALLS

Purpose
- Define space in your landscape
- Making space more useful, beautiful and safe
- Correct problems with the erosion of landscape.
- Prevention of water runoff.

Factors that affect design
- Soil conditions
- Weather patterns
- Slope
- Drainage

Building permits
- May be required by city codes for walls exceeding specified heights

Structural elements
- Foundations
- Reinforcing rods

CONCEPTS

Footing drain (foundation drains and "weeping or seepage tile) — Pipe with holes that allows water in the ground to enter it
- Used to remove water in the ground adjacent to the foundation and/or basement walls

Permit — Required for a retaining wall whenever the wall exceeds 4' in height, measured from grade at the bottom of the wall to the top of the wall
- Generally required where there is a surcharge (or load) on the wall or on walls higher than 3'.

Reinforced Embankment — The use of various natural and man-made materials to strengthen a mound of earth, stone or other materials built to hold back water or to support a roadway.

Weep hole — A hole which allows for drainage of entrapped water from any rigid wall
- Designed to relieve pressure caused by excessive water behind retaining wall

Rough Carpentry

The initial stage of carpentry when all components that won't be seen after the second finishing phase are assembled

Wood framing — Use of lumber for the structural members of a building, such as studs, joists, and rafters

Furring — To shim out and provide a level fastening surface for a wall or ceiling

Grounds — Guides used around openings and at the floorline to strike off plaster. They can consist of narrow strips of wood or of wide sub-jambs at interior doorways. They provide a level plaster line for installation of casing and other trim.

Nailers — A piece of lumber secured to non-nailable decks and walls by bolts or other means, which provides a suitable backing onto which roof components may be mechanically fastened

Blocking — Small wood pieces to brace framing members or to provide a nailing base for gypsum board or paneling

Security Systems

Method of protecting people and property using various types of devices

Alarm Systems
- Use control panels, many types of sensors, door and window contacts that detect break-ins or unauthorized entry
- Can be mounted on doors or windows
- Sounds an alarm
- Monitors alarm condition
- Notifies proper authorities
- Alerts people to fire

Types of sensors
- Motion detectors
- Heat detectors
- Microwave beams
- Infrared beams
- Pressure sensors

Integrated computer-based security system
- Provides access control to designated areas within a site or facility using both proximity and magnetic stripe technology
  - By swiping the card through a reader
  - By holding card in close proximity to the reader

Digital technology in CCTV applications and remote video surveillance
- Transmit images to a modulator
- Modulator assigns each camera to an unused channel of cable TV system.
- Can be linked to a remote monitoring system that feeds the pictures to a secure Web site

Remote monitoring via the Web
- Internet Monitoring Systems with a video camera that's wireless
- Has its own built-in Web server and IP address
- Shoot images to any Web-enabled device (cell phone, computer, pager), without the help of a computer

Signs

With any project that is classified as signs, the limitations of zoning laws that affect the requirements and occupancy of the land take precedence over the regulations of the building codes.

GENERAL REQUIREMENTS

Signs projecting from a building or extending over public property
- Maintain a clear height of 9' (2743 mm) above the sidewalk and all such signs extend not more than within 18" (457 mm) of the curb line
- Construct as to leave a clear space of not less than 6' (1829 mm) between the roof level and the lowest part of the sign
- Construct entirely of steel construction, including the upright supports and braces, except that only the ornamental molding and battens behind the steel facing and the decorative latticework may be of wood construction.
- Have bearing plates that distribute the load directly to or upon masonry walls, steel roof girders, columns or beams
- Not have a roof sign with a tight or solid surface at any point over 24' (7315 mm)
- Erect open roof signs in which the uniform open area is not less than 40% of total gross area to a height of 75' (22.9 m) on buildings of Type I or Type II construction and on other type buildings to a height of 40' (12.2 m)
- Secure thoroughly to the building upon which they are installed, erected or constructed by iron, metal anchors, bolts, supports, chains, stranded cables, steel rods or braces
- Maintain in good condition
- Have at least 5' (1524 mm) clearance between the vertical supports thereof. No portion of any roof sign structure shall project beyond an exterior wall.

TYPES

Closed sign — More than 50% of the entire area is solid or tightly enclosed or covered.
Ground sign — Supported by uprights or braces in or upon the ground surface
Projecting sign — Display sign which is attached directly to the building wall, and which extends more than 15" (381 mm) from the face of the wall.
Roof sign — Erected, constructed and maintained above the roof of the building.

Wall sign — Painted on or attached directly to a fence or on the surface of masonry, concrete, frame or other approved building walls, and which extends not more than 15" (381 mm) from the face of the fence or wall

SIGNAGE

Character Proportion
- Width-to-height ratio between 3:5 and Character Height
- Size according to the viewing distance from which they are to be read
- The minimum height is measured using an upper case X.
- Lower case characters are permitted.

Height above Finished Floor
- Have 80" (2030 mm) minimum clear head room
- Have a barrier to warn blind/visually-impaired persons if vertical clearance of an area adjoining an accessible route is reduced to less than 80"

Minimum Character Height
- 3" (75 mm) minimum

Raised and Brailled Characters
- Raise 1/32" (0.8 mm) minimum, upper case, sans serif or simple serif type
- Accompany with Grade 2 Braille
- At least 5/8" (16 mm) high, but no higher than 2" (50 mm)

Pictorial Symbol Signs (Pictograms)
- Accompany by the equivalent verbal description placed directly below the pictogram
- 6" (152 mm) border dimension minimum in height

Finish and Contrast
- Eggshell, matte, or other non-glare finish
- Contrast with their background -- either light characters on a dark background or dark characters on a light background

Mounting Location
- Installed on the wall adjacent to the latch side of the door
- Placed on the nearest adjacent wall where there is no wall space to the latch side of the door

Mounting height
- 60" (1525 mm) above the finish floor to the centerline of the sign
- So that a person may approach within 3" (76 mm) of signage without encountering protruding objects or standing within the swing of a door

Structural Loads

A building must be designed to withstand various types of loads. Model building codes and engineering standards are the best available guidance for identifying the basic load combinations that should be used to design buildings

CONCEPTS

Auxiliary loads — Dynamic live loads such as those induced by cranes and material handling system

Concentrated load — Applied to a structural element that can be considered as being applied at a point rather than being applied uniformly across a span
- Example: Heater unit hung from a beam

Dead load — The load attributed to the building itself (the weight of the beams, floor slabs, and partitions)

Dimensionally stable — Any building material that does not alter shape appreciably (as in bowing or twisting) due to changes in temperature, humidity and loading conditions

Design load — Loads expressly specified in the contract documents which the building system is designed to safely resist

Lateral loads — Horizontal force acting on the structure
- Example: Earth pressure against a retaining wall

Live load — A member (furniture and people) that is not permanent and is likely to be moved at some point in the life of the structure
- Example: Anything that will cause a vibration

Load-bearing — A structure that supports weight

Seismic load — A load on a structure caused by movement of the earth relative to the structure during an earthquake

Snow load — Expressed in weight of accumulated snow on a square foot of ground

Uniform load — Distributed over a structural member, floor, or column without any concentrated loading condition (Pounds per square foot; pounds per square inch)

Wind load — A dynamic lateral load, which acts on the building façade as a uniformly varying load

DEFLECTION

Result of structural member bent by its own weight
Also, the amount of displacement resulting from this bending

Code on allowable deflection of structural members
- Maximum deflection limits are set by building codes.
- Live loads are set by code.
- Expressed as a fraction; clear span in inches (L) over a given number

Factors that influence
- Depth of structural members
- Higher stiffness (E value)
  - E is a ratio that relates the amount a given load causes a material to deform. A material with a higher E value is stiffer.

- Higher strength rating (Fb)The higher the Fb the stronger the wood
- Species of wood
- Lumber grade

Duration of load
- Full-time loading (floor joists) serves as the benchmark value.
- Benchmark values are multiplied by 1.15 to yield snow-load values and by 1.25 for 7-day loading.
- Tables automatically handle this adjustment.

CODE

From the ICC International Residential Code

Minimum uniformly distributed live load
- <u>Use</u>   <u>Live Load</u>
  Decks   40
  Stairs   40

Allowable deflection of structural members

<u>Structural Member</u>	<u>Allowable Deflection</u>
Rafters with slope	> 3/12 and no ceiling attached L/180
Floors and plastered ceilings	L/360
All other structural members	L/240

Floor joist with L360 deflection limits design criteria
- Deflection - For 40 PSF live load
- Limited to span in inches divided by 360
- Strength - Live load of 40 psf plus dead load of 10 psf determines the required bending design value.
-
Design values for joists and rafters visually graded lumber
- Use Fb values where repetitive members are spaced not more than 24"
- For wider spacing, the Fb values shall be reduced 13%.
- Values for surfaced dry or surfaced green lumber apply at 19% maximum moisture content in use.

This section tests your knowledge of the design and construction process.

Termite Control

Building design may contribute to termite invasion. A certified pest management professional is required when treating or preventing termite infestations.

Prevention
- Keep all substructural wood at least 12" above the soil beneath the building
- Keep foundation areas well ventilated and dry

- Seal openings, such as knotholes and cracks, to discourage the entry of winged drywood termites.
- Reduce chances of infestation by removing or protecting any wood in contact with the soil.
- Inspect porches and other structural or foundation wood for signs of termites. Look for and remove tree stumps, stored lumber, untreated fence posts, and buried scrap wood near the structure that may attract termites

Treatment

- **Chemical Treatment**
  o Most common treatment type available for Subterranean termites
  o Have technician place termiticide in the soil on both sides of all foundation elements to create a protective barrier around the property
  o Trench the soil and inject termiticide beneath it at 16" intervals.
  o Drill into hollow masonry block foundations and inject termiticide into the block voids.
  o Generally good for 5 years

- **Baiting Systems**
  o Fast becoming a popular method of treatment for subterranean termites
  o Place cellulose (wood material) bait stations at strategic locations around the perimeter of the home for worker termites to locate and leave special scent trails to summon their mates to the food source
  o Replace cellulose material with a chemical inhibitor which retards the molting process in termites, preventing them from growing. The carrier termites then bring the chemical back to the colony and causing the carrier and the rest of the colony will die.

Wood Preservatives

Voluntary standards for preservative treatment are developed by the American Wood-Preservers Association. The AWPA's Use Category System allows identification of treated lumber according to end use or exposure (such as "above ground" or "ground contact") regardless of the specific wood species and treatment process.

These treatments keep the wood from rotting and repel termites.

Alkaline Copper Quat (ACQ)
- Fixed preservative approved for full exposure to above ground, ground contact, and freshwater applications.

Copper Azole (CA)
- Fixed preservative approved for full exposure to above ground, ground contact, and freshwater applications.

Sodium Borate (SBX)
- Diffusible preservative approved only for above ground applications that are continuously protected from liquid water, such as sill plates and other enclosed structural framing.

Chromated Copper Arsenate (CCA)

- As of December 31, 2003 CCA has been withdrawn for most residential consumer-use treated lumber applications.
- CCA treatment will continue to be allowed for certain industrial, agricultural, foundation, and marine applications.

Most treated wood products have a life expectancy of 20 – 25 years.

Math

As with most licensure tests, the ability to utilize basic math formulas is a necessary skill.

BASIC MATH SKILLS

The candidate must be able to do the following math operations.
- Compute using decimals, fractions, and percents and convert from one to another
- Use and convert between the British and metric systems of measurement
- Use formulas involving perimeter, area, volume, and percent
- Solve simple equations of the form "x + a = b" and "ax = b"
- Compute ratios
- Solve proportions
- Compute the perimeter and area of various plane figures including rectangles, squares, triangles, parallelograms, trapezoids, and circles
- Apply the Pythagorean Theorem
- Compute the volume and surface area of various solids, including rectangular parallelepipeds, cylinders, and spheres
- Measure distances using direct measurement and estimation
- Perform calculations involved in sales, including discount and mark-up
- Solve landscape construction problems involving ties, bricks, blocks, and wall stone
- Perform mulch, soil, and stone calculations
- Perform calculations involving seed mixtures, sod, fertilizer, and chemical mixtures
- Construct a scale drawing using an architect's scale
- Complete a bid sheet (estimate) for a landscaping project

COMMON FORMULAS USED IN SOLUTIONS

Basic Grading Formula

G = Grade	decimal
D = Difference in elevation	ft.
L = Length	ft.

- Grade formula

$$G = \frac{D}{L}$$

- Difference in Elevation Formula

$$D = GL$$

- Length Formula

$$L = \frac{D}{G}$$

Cross-Slope Formula

Df = Length of the deflection   ft
CS = Desired cross slope   decimal
W = Width of the plane surface at cross slope   ft
LG = Longitudinal grade of the plane surface   decimal

$$Df = \frac{(CS)W}{LG}$$

Rational Method Formula

Q = Water volume, or flow ft^3/sec
C = Coefficient of runoff   decimal
I = Intensity of rainfall   in/hr
A = Area   ac

$$Q = CIA$$

Calculating slope

% (decimal number) = vertical distance: horizontal distance
Vertical distance = horizontal distance x % (decimal number)
Horizontal distance = vertical distance: % (decimal number)

The following formula calculates the length of the slope:
H = horizontal distance   ft
V = vertical distance   ft
S = slope distance   ft

$$H^2 + V^2 = S^2$$
$$\text{or } S = \sqrt{H^2 + V^2}$$

Examples:

Gentle slope: We have a horizontal distance of 25' and a vertical distance of 3'
- The calculation is: (25 x 25) + (3 x 3) = 625 + 9 = 634
- The square root of 634 is 25.18
- The slope distance is 25.18'.

Steep slope: We have a horizontal distance of 25' and a vertical distance of 25'.
- The calculation is: (25 x 25) + (25 x 25) = 625 + 625 = 1250
- The square root of 1250 is 35.35
- The slope distance is 35.35'.

Note: The steeper the slope, the greater the difference between actual horizontal distance and slope distance.

Calculating Ratios

Ratios are always expressed as horizontal distance: vertical distance.
The actual distance measurements are not important when expressing ratios only the relationship between them.
- If the horizontal distance is 5.75 times as long as the vertical distance is high, the ratio is 5.75: 1.
- If the vertical distance is 9.97 times as high as the horizontal distance is long, the ratio is 1: 9.97.
- To arrive at the other figure, simply divide the larger number by the smaller number.
- Example: If the horizontal distance is 75', and the vertical distance is 5', divide 75 by 5 = 15, making the ration 15: 1
- Example: If the horizontal distance is 10' and the vertical distance is 27', divide 27 by 10 = 2.7, making the ratio 1: 2.7

Note: The higher the second number, the steeper the slope.

Calculating Percentages

To figure out the percentage of a grade, take the vertical distance and divide it by the horizontal distance, regardless of which figure is bigger.
- Example: If the horizontal distance is 75', and the vertical distance is 5', divide the height by the horizontal distance, 5 divided by 75 = 0.066 or 6.6%
- Example: If the horizontal distance is 10' and the vertical distance is 27', divide 27 by 10 = 2.7 or 270%
- A 45º angle (equal height and distance) would be 100%

Note: The higher the percentage, the steeper the slope.

Practice Test

Practice Questions

1. What is the purpose of a MasterFormat?
    a. provide a standard to organize specifications and important paperwork for a project
    b. provide a standard to codify all industry abbreviations and acronyms
    c. provide intermediate skill training for employees who want to master higher level skills
    d. provide a uniform format for all written communications to employees

2. Which of the following includes an overhead view of spaces on a floor of a building?
    a. site plan
    b. architectural plan
    c. plan view
    d. architectural schedule

3. Which of the following is a requirement for a contract to be valid?
    a. Both parties must be at least 25 years of age.
    b. There must be an exchange of a thing in return for a promise of another thing.
    c. It must be witnessed by a notary public.
    d. An escrow account must be used.

4. A builder agrees in a contract to use a certain kind of interior paint. However, he delays purchasing the paint until absolutely necessary, hoping the price will go down. When the building is nearly completed and is ready to be painted, he discovers that the paint is no longer being manufactured. He then uses a lower-cost brand of paint without notifying the client. This builder has committed:
    a. nonfeasance
    b. misfeasance
    c. malfeasance
    d. disfeasance

5. In some contracts, both parties agree to give up their right to go to court in case of conflicts, and instead use a disinterested third party to settle any possible disputes. This method of resolving disputes is known as:
    a. mediation
    b. binding arbitration
    c. nonbinding arbitration
    d. civic disposition

6. Which of the following is the most important factor in determining how much water the soil can hold?
    a. the kind of soil
    b. the average amount of rainfall in the area
    c. the season
    d. the climate

7. Which of the following is used for a minor change to the requirements of the contract?
   a. field order
   b. change order
   c. addendum
   d. stipulation

8. Which kind of contract is appropriate when there's some uncertainty as to the scope of the project?
   a. bid with reserve
   b. stipulated sum
   c. unit price
   d. cost plus fee

9. On a request for proposal, it would be inappropriate for an entity to ask a firm to provide which of the following:
   a. company financial information
   b. references from previous customers
   c. education/work histories of employees
   d. medical records of employees

10. A Notice of Substantial Completion can be issued when ___% of construction is complete.
   a. 95
   b. 85
   c. 75
   d. 70

11. Which of the following allows a landscape architect who is licensed in a state to practice in another state without having to pass a licensing exam in the second state?
   a. Title act
   b. Practice act
   c. Reciprocity agreement
   d. Sunrise law

12. Which of these are required in order for a change order to be valid?
   a. a signature from the contractor or an authorized agent
   b. a signature from the client or an authorized agent
   c. signatures from both parties or their authorized agents
   d. signatures from both parties or their authorized agents and from the local building authority

13. Which one of the following is not a primary concern addressed by LEED?
   a. energy efficiency
   b. material selection
   c. indoor environmental quality
   d. fire hazard reduction

14. During your initial site analysis, you notice a lot of duffage. This could:
   a. be a fire hazard
   b. mean the site lacks sufficient drainage
   c. represent a hurdle to getting EPA clearance
   d. be due to soil erosion

15. Site analysis and design should take into account human factors, which include:
    a. plant species proposed for us in landscaping
    b. environmental history of the site
    c. cost of construction
    d. all of the above

16. Lowering the elevation of a grade is known as:
    a. making a fill
    b. cutting a fill
    c. making a cut
    d. filling the cut

17. Under ordinary circumstances, the EPA requires a minimum distance of ___ feet between the water main and any drain, sewer, or sewer connection:
    a. 10
    b. 20
    c. 25
    c. 50

18. Trees that grow ___ feet or higher should not be planted near power lines.
    a. 10
    b. 15
    c. 25
    d. 30

19. Utility easements are not placed:
    a. alongside roads
    b. along rear lot lines
    c. between lots
    d. underneath roads

20. Having a lot of windows facing _____ maximizes solar access in winter and reduces heating costs.
    a. east
    b. west
    c. south
    d. north

21. Which of the following is not a policy of the ASLA Code of Environmental Ethics?
    a. Transgenic plants should be used whenever possible to reduce the need for pesticides.
    b. Wetlands should be protected, preserved and enhanced.
    c. Public park space should be expanded for the benefit of all people.
    d. Maintaining the visual environment of a site is as important as maintaining its natural resources.

22. Which of the following is another name for firescaping?
    a. flatlining
    b. defensible space
    c. fire spacing
    d. aridscaping

23. CPTED is about using landscape design to:
    a. reduce environmental dangers
    b. minimize earthquake damage
    c. reduce the incidence of crime
    d. focus attention on natural features

24. A crowned surface provides the fastest water removal, since the distance water has to travel is reduced by ___%.
    a. 25
    b. 33
    c. 50
    d. 75

25. The design principle that refers to the aesthetic integration of diverse elements is:
    a. balance
    b. form
    c. harmony
    d. proportion

26. The concept of unity in landscape design requires:
    a. proximity
    b. continuation
    c. continuity
    d. all of the above

27. Which of the following is a major strategy of CPTED?
    a. low population density
    b. territorial reinforcement
    c. walkability
    d. high population density

28. A high risk flood zone is an area which has a greater than ____% chance of flooding in any given year.
    a. 1
    b. 3
    c. 5
    d. 7

29. Which kind of sprinkler system is best for medium to large outdoor areas?
    a. spray pop-ups
    b. gear-driven rotors
    c. impact heads
    d. large turf rotors

30. Which of the following lighting techniques is used to create special effects?
    a. backlighting
    b. uplighting
    c. downlighting
    d. moonlighting

31. Which of the following exterior lamps have the longest life but the lowest efficiency?
    a. high pressure sodium lamps
    b. metal halide lamps
    c. low voltage incandescent lamps
    d. mercury vapor lamps

32. Which of the following is the conceptual layout for a site?
    a. master plan
    b. staking plan
    c. site plan
    d. blueprint

33. The coordinate system is used for locating the following site elements except:
    a. light poles
    b. drain inlets
    c. parking lots
    d. manholes

34. Which of these is not typically a component of a constructed wetland?
    a. gravel layer
    b. clay layer
    c. impermeable layer
    d. vegetation zone

35. Which of the following are given the lowest priority when preparing a layout plan?
    a. non-determined features
    b. semi-fixed features
    c. adjustive features
    d. fixed features

36. After runoff water passes through a wetland, it is:
    a. a little more polluted
    b. much less polluted
    c. a little less polluted
    d. about as polluted as it was when it entered the wetland

37. A shaded walkway featuring an open lattice between vertical posts is:
    a. a pergola
    b. a terrace
    c. a gazebo
    d. an atrium

38. Which of the following is a commonly used penetrating finish?
    a. lacquer
    b. semi-transparent stain
    c. shellac
    d. polyurethane

39. Deck footings do all of the following except:
    a. prevent frost heave
    b. eliminate settling
    c. eliminate slipping
    d. protect against termites

40. Barrier-type curbs are not recommended for projects with design speeds above __ MPH.
    a. 25
    b. 30
    c. 40
    d. 45

41. In 2012, the USDA introduced a new Plant Hardiness Zone map. How many zones does the new USDA map include?
    a. 12
    b. 13
    c. 14
    d. 15

42. Specified daily charges deducted from moneys otherwise payable to the contractor for each day the contractor fails to meet a milestone and/or contract completion date are known as:
    a. liquidated damages
    b. forbearance fees
    c. non-performance assessments
    d. good-til-completion payments

43. Which of the following can be used to control the erosive power of water on road surfaces?
    a. downsloping
    b. upsloping
    c. insloping
    d. outsloping

44. Which of the following is not an OSHA standard that applies to landscaping and horticulture?
    a. SIC Code 0781
    b. SIC Code 0782
    c. SIC Code 0783
    d. SIC Code 0784

45. Which government agency sets standards concerning the development of historic buildings and sites?
    a. Department of Housing and Urban Development
    b. Department of the Interior
    c. Department of Commerce
    d. Environmental Protection Agency

46. Which of the following is the standard contract between a landscape architect and a client?
    a. A511TM
    b. AIA Document B151
    c. AIA Document B141
    d. AIA Document C112

47. Which government agency oversees the protection of wetlands?
    a. EPA
    b. Department of Commerce
    c. Department of the Interior
    d. Army Corps of Engineers

48. According to the Americans with Disabilities Act, in general, the maximum grade of an accessible walking path should be ___%.
    a. 3
    b. 4
    c. 5
    d. 6

49. Which bikeway provides for shared use with pedestrian or motor traffic and has identifying signage?
    a. Class I Bikeway
    b. Class II Bikeway
    c. Class III Bikeway
    d. Class IV Bikeway

50. Who is generally considered to be the father of landscape architecture as we know it?
    a. George Washington Vanderbilt
    b. Frederick Law Olmsted
    c. Calvert Vaux
    d. Daniel Burnham

Answers and Explanations

1. A: MasterFormat is a standard for organizing specifications and important paperwork on construction projects, either institutional or commercial. It is used in both the US and Canada. Developed by the Construction Specifications Institute (CS) and Construction Specifications Canada, it used to have 16 divisions. However, as the number of construction materials and techniques began to expand, the number of divisions was increased, and there are now 50.

2. C: A plan view includes an overhead view of the spaces on a specific floor. It also indicates the length, width and various heights of the structure and floor elevations, and may also contain details on a specific portion of work.

3. B: A valid contract can only be made between parties who are legally old enough to be held responsible for their actions, which is 18 years of age. One party must give or do something or promise to give or do something benefitting the other party, in exchange for something else, usually money. A contract that involves illegal activity is by definition not valid. Using an escrow account is not necessary, nor is having the contract attested to by a notary public.

4. B: The contractor has committed misfeasance. Nonfeasance occurs when a party agrees to do something, but never follows through at all. If the builder and his crew simply stopped showing up halfway through the project's completion that would be nonfeasance. Misfeasance consists of performing agreed upon work, but in an improper way, which is what this case falls under. Malfeasance is to commit acts clearly intended to harm the other party's interests. If the builder had set fire to the building in order to get out of paying a penalty for not using the agreed upon paint, that would be malfeasance.

5. B: When two parties agree to give up their right to go to court to settle disputes but instead rely on a neutral, third party to resolve the problem, this is known as binding arbitration. If they agree to let a neutral third party make a decision, but reserve the right to go to court if they don't like the arbitrator's ruling, that is nonbinding arbitration. In mediation, parties negotiate their disputes with each other, using a neutral third party, or mediator, to help guide and oversee the process.

6. A: The biggest factor when it comes to how much water soil can hold is the kind of soil. Soil contains pore spaces, or little holes, that can hold water. The size of the holes depends on the soil type, and the size of the holes determines how much water soil can hold.

7. A: During the life of a large construction project, changes to the requirements of the contract will sometimes be necessary. This can occur as a result of a large number of factors. For fairly substantial changes, a change order must take place. For minor changes, a field order will suffice.

8. C: When there is uncertainty about how big the scope of a project will actually turn out to be, the best contract option is price per unit.

9. D: An entity would be out of line asking for employee medical records, but would not be out of line asking for any of the information listed in the other answer choices. An entity soliciting bids wants to be sure that a company has the financial stability to be able to deliver on their contract, so financial information is certainly a concern. It would also be appropriate to want to hear from

previous customers, and to know what kind of education and/or work experience a bidder's employees will bring to the project.

10. A: 95% of the construction must be completed in order for the local government building authority to issue a Notice of Substantial Completion.

11. C: A reciprocity agreement allows a landscape architect who is licensed in a state to practice in another state without being required to pass a licensing exam in the second state. These agreements are called reciprocal, because the agreements work both ways – state A agrees to recognize state B's licensed landscape architects, and state B agrees to honor landscape architects who have been granted licenses in state A.

12. C: A change order represents a substantial change to the contract, unlike a field order, which covers minor changes. Because of this, both parties must give their signature showing their approval of the change order, which then becomes the operative contract.

13. D: Fire hazard reduction is not one of the primary reasons for following LEED guidelines. LEED stands for Leadership in Energy and Environmental Design. It is the nationally accepted benchmark for the design, construction, and operation of high performance green buildings. LEED promotes a whole-building approach to sustainability by recognizing performance in these key areas of human and environmental health: Sustainable site development | Water savings/Energy efficiency | Materials selection | Indoor environmental quality.

14. A: Duffage is a term that refers to plant droppings on the ground, such as dead leaves, dead fiber/bark, dead blooms, etc. If it builds up in sufficient quantities it can represent a fire hazard on a site.

15. A: Human factors (ergonomics) refers to the study of how humans behave physically and psychologically in relation to particular environments, products, or services. These include choice of materials, plant species selected for a particular landscape, how land is going to be used - outdoor living, playing, gardening and household servicing, etc. It also includes views and proximity of goods and services, but not the environmental history of the site, or the cost of construction.

16. C: Lowering the elevation of a grade is known as making a cut. Raising the elevation of the ground is known as making a fill. The determination of earthwork quantities is based upon field cross-sections taken in a specified manner before and after excavation.

17. A: EPA standards state that the water main must be located at least 10' horizontally from any existing or proposed drain, storm sewer, sanitary sewer, combined sewer, or sewer service connection, unless local conditions prevent a lateral separation of 10'. If it is not possible to obtain 10' separation the Agency may approve construction in which the water main invert must be 18" above the crown of the sewer. In parallel situations where it is not possible to obtain the lateral or vertical separation, then the Agency may approve construction in which the sewer is constructed of water main equivalent pipe and pressure tested to the maximum expected surcharge head before backfilling.

18. C: As a general rule, trees that grow 25' or higher should not be planted near power lines. Trees with far-reaching root systems should not be planted near sewer lines or septic systems. Roots can easily force their way between sewer tiles, blocking or breaking them. Inappropriately placed large

trees can damage sidewalks and curbs, in addition to phone, water, sewer and electric lines. They also can affect traffic visibility.

19. D: Utility easements are strips of land used by utility companies to construct and maintain overhead electric, telephone and cable television lines and underground electric, water, and sewer, telephone, and cable television lines. The property owner owns all of the land including the utility easements, but utilities have a right to access that portion of land which has been designated a utility easement. Utility easements are usually created at the time a plat for a new development is designed. Utility easements almost always exist along roadways and along rear lot lines, and sometimes exist between two lots. They are never beneath roads.

20. C: For maximum solar access during the cold seasons, windows should face south. Of course, this is only true in the northern hemisphere; in the southern hemisphere, windows should face north for maximum solar access during the cold seasons.

21. A: The ASLA Code of Environmental Ethics states that the use of transgenic (genetically modified) plants should be avoided until such time as we have clear evidence that they won't lead to adverse environmental effects. The other three choices are all official policies of the ASLA Code of Environmental Ethics.

22. B: Defensible space is another name for firescaping, which refers to designing landscapes in such a way as to reduce the likelihood of a fire starting or spreading.

23. C: CPTED stands for crime prevention through environmental design. The way outdoor areas are built can have a significant impact on the levels of crime in an area. Although no studies have proven that using the principles of CPTED actually reduces crime, many of them are "common sense," and they also tend to make legitimate users of a site feel safer, which is usually a positive.

24. C: A crowned surface provides the fastest water removal since the distance water has to travel is cut in half. The crowned surface slopes at 3 to 10 percent from either side of the road centerline. Crowned surfaces and any associated cross drains or dips are difficult to maintain. Water has to be controlled on both sides of the road through a ditch line and stable areas have to be provided for runoff water. Ballast thickness is typically the largest in the center in order to achieve the correct crown shape.

25. C: The design principle that refers to the aesthetic integration of diverse elements is Harmony.

26. D: To create a landscape in which all the elements appear to belong together requires:
- Proximity - placing elements together to form a grouping
- Repetition - replicating features such as shape, color or texture.
- Continuation - creating a line or edge that carries the viewer's eye throughout the space
- Continuity - visual relationships between two or more designs

27. B: The four strategies of CPTED are:
- Natural Surveillance - features that maximize visibility of people, lighted parking areas and building entrances, doors and windows that look out on to streets and parking areas, front porches
- Territorial Reinforcement - features that define property lines and distinguish private spaces from public spaces using landscape plantings, pavement designs, gateway treatments, and "CPTED" fences
- Natural Access Control - streets, sidewalks, building entrances and neighborhood gateways to define public routes and discourage access to private areas
- Target Hardening - features that prohibit entry or access: window locks, dead bolts, interior door hinges

28. A: The Federal Emergency Management Agency (FEMA) has set the 1% standard for defining a high risk flood zone. That is, any area which has a higher than one in a hundred annual chance of flooding is defined as a high risk flood zone.

29. B: Gear-driven rotors are used for medium- to large-scale areas, replacing older impact heads in many situations. Their radius can vary from 15' - 70'. Medium-sized gear-driven rotors apply water at a much slower rate than spray pop-ups.

30. A: Backlighting, or silhouette lighting, provides a special effect by illuminating a fairly large surface (like a wall) using a wash light fixture.

31. D: Mercury vapor lamps have the longest life but the lowest energy efficiency. They are recommended for use as street lighting in residential areas where lower levels of lighting may be desirable and color rendition is a secondary. They are also a good choice for landscape accent lighting.

32. A: A master plan is a conceptual layout for a site. It outlines a logical phased growth plan and indicates the maximum potential usage of a site. A master plan is not an attempt to generate a floor plan for every future project. A master plan can be used for presentations and fund raisers.

33. C: The coordinate system is used for the location of such site elements as building corners, corners of all paved areas, light pole locations, tops and bottoms of all steps, radius points, length of walls and fences and their corner posts, as well as the and location of utility structures such as drain inlets, manholes and headwalls

34. B: Usually, the constructed wetland has three primary components: an impermeable layer (generally clay), a gravel layer that provides a substrate (i.e., an area that provides nutrients and support) for the root zone, and an above-surface vegetation zone.

35. A: The order of priority for features when preparing a layout plan, from highest to lowest is: fixed, semi-fixed, adjustive, and non-determined.

36. B: After being slowed by the wetland, polluted runoff water moves through finding its way around plants and through small spaces in the soil. While it moves, the nutrients are absorbed by the plant. By the time, the water leaves the wetland it is much cleaner than when it entered.

37. A: A shaded walkway featuring an open lattice between vertical posts is a pergola.

38. B: The most common types of penetrating finishes are water repellents, water repellents with preservatives, and semi-transparent stains. The other three answer choices are surface finishes.

39. D: Footings eliminate settling and slippage, and help protect posts and beams from direct contact with the earth. Footings also prevent frost heave. Footings are typically placed 6" below the frost line. The frost line is the maximum depth where the ground will freeze in the winter. Many municipalities have code regulations on footing depth and width, type, and fill material. Footing should rise at least 3" above ground level to keep the post dry.

40. C: Barrier-type curbs are not recommended for projects with design speeds above 40 mph (65 km/h).

41. B: The new Plant Hardiness Zone map from the United States Department of Agriculture contains 13 zones. The map is used to determine which plants are best able to survive and thrive in a particular location, based on the temperature extremes of the area.

42. A: Specified daily charges deducted from moneys otherwise payable to the contractor for each day the contractor fails to meet a milestone and/or contract completion date are known as liquidated damages. Liquidated damages are a contract based remedy for late completion of the contract. It must be agreed to by the parties in the construction contract.

43. C: Insloping is used where a more reliable drainage system is required such as on permanent roads, roads with high anticipated traffic volumes and/or loads, or in areas with sensitive soils or severe climatic conditions. Insloping is achieved by grading the road surface towards the uphill side of the road at a 3 to 5 percent grade. Water draining from insloped road surfaces is collected and carried along the inside of the road either on the road surface itself or more commonly in a ditch line.

44. D: Landscape and horticultural services encompass a wide range of services. Included in this category are companies engaged in landscape design and architecture; soil preparation and grading; irrigation systems; tree, shrub and lawn planting; hardscape construction including: retaining walls, pathways and patios; lawn care and landscape maintenance; arborist services including tree trimming and line clearance.
Landscape and horticultural services can be separated into three main segments:
- SIC Code 0781 - Landscape Counseling and Planning (Landscape Design and Consultation)
- SIC Code 0782 - Lawn and Garden Services (Landscape Installation and Maintenance)
- SIC Code 0783 – Ornamental Shrub and Tree Services (Tree Pruning and Arboriculture)

Each area must comply with the general industry standards (29 CFR 1910) and Construction industry standards (29 CFR 1926).

45. B: The Secretary of the Interior promulgates the Standards for Architectural and Engineering Documentation. These standards concern the development of documentation for historic buildings, sites, structures and objects. This documentation, which usually consists of measured drawings, photographs and written data, provides important information on a property's significance for use by scholars, researchers, preservationists, architects, engineers and others interested in preserving and understanding historic properties.

46. C: AIA contract forms typically used depending upon the scope of the project include:
- AIA Document B141, Standard Form of Agreement Between Owner and Architect
- AIA Document B151, Abbreviated Form of Agreement Between Owner and Architect for Construction (condensed version)
- AIA Document B163, Standard Form of Agreement Between Owner and Architect for Designated Services, is used to employ the designated services approach. B163 provides a range of 83 separate architectural, interiors, and construction management services from which to choose. The owner pays only for the services necessary for the project's success, and the architect can effectively measure the firm's time and resources.
- AIA Document A201-1997, General Conditions of the Contract for Construction
- A511TM, Guide for Supplementary Conditions

47. A: EPA has a number of programs for wetland conservation, restoration, and monitoring. EPA, along with the U.S. Army Corps of Engineers (Corps), establishes environmental standards for reviewing permits for discharges that affect wetlands, such as residential development, roads, and levees. Under Section 404 of the Clean Water Act, the Corps issues permits that meet environmental standards (after allowing the public to comment). EPA works with a variety of other federal agencies to protect and restore wetlands, including the U.S. Fish and Wildlife Service, the U.S. Department of Agriculture, and the National Marine Fisheries Service.

48. C: The ADA has several requirements to help ensure ease of access for all non-motorized travelers, including those in wheelchairs and motorized scooters. Some of these requirements are as follows:
- In most cases, a minimum 3' wide clear zone must be provided along a route with obstacles.
- Railings should be between 34" and 38". If children are the primary users of a facility, a 2nd set of handrails, no taller than 28", should be installed.
- Generally, grades along an accessible route walking path should not exceed 1:20 or 5%.
- Ramp slopes should not exceed 1:12 or 8.33% in new facilities.
- If a designated accessible route has a grade greater than 5%, it is considered a ramp and must have handrails and landings.

49. C: Bikeways are generally described by as being one of three basic types:
• Class I Bikeway is variously called a bike path or multi-use trail and provides for bicycle travel on a right of way completely separated from any street or highway.
• Class II Bikeway is referred to as a bike lane and provides a striped lane for one-way travel on a street or highway.
• Class III Bikeway is referred to as a bike route and provides for shared use with pedestrian or motor vehicle traffic and is identified only by signing.

50. B: Frederick Law Olsted (1822-1903) is generally regarded as the father of landscape architecture. He designed many of America's state parks, and is known for many other iconic designs, such as Central Park and Prospect Park in New York City.

Secret Key #1 – Time Is Your Greatest Enemy

Pace Yourself

Wear a watch. At the beginning of the test, check the time (or start a chronometer on your watch to count the minutes), and check the time after every few questions to make sure you are "on schedule."

If you are forced to speed up, do it efficiently. Usually one or more answer choices can be eliminated without too much difficulty. Above all, don't panic. Don't speed up and just begin guessing at random choices. By pacing yourself, and continually monitoring your progress against your watch, you will always know exactly how far ahead or behind you are with your available time. If you find that you are one minute behind on the test, don't skip one question without spending any time on it, just to catch back up. Take 15 fewer seconds on the next four questions, and after four questions you'll have caught back up. Once you catch back up, you can continue working each problem at your normal pace.

Furthermore, don't dwell on the problems that you were rushed on. If a problem was taking up too much time and you made a hurried guess, it must be difficult. The difficult questions are the ones you are most likely to miss anyway, so it isn't a big loss. It is better to end with more time than you need than to run out of time.

Lastly, sometimes it is beneficial to slow down if you are constantly getting ahead of time. You are always more likely to catch a careless mistake by working more slowly than quickly, and among very high-scoring test takers (those who are likely to have lots of time left over), careless errors affect the score more than mastery of material.

Secret Key #2 – Guessing Is Not Guesswork

You probably know that guessing is a good idea - unlike other standardized tests, there is no penalty for getting a wrong answer. Even if you have no idea about a question, you still have a 20-25% chance of getting it right.

Most test takers do not understand the impact that proper guessing can have on their score. Unless you score extremely high, guessing will significantly contribute to your final score.

Monkeys Take the Test

What most test takers don't realize is that to insure that 20-25% chance, you have to guess randomly. If you put 20 monkeys in a room to take this test, assuming they answered once per question and behaved themselves, on average they would get 20-25% of the questions correct. Put 20 test takers in the room, and the average will be much lower among guessed questions. Why?
1. The test writers intentionally write deceptive answer choices that "look" right. A test taker has no idea about a question, so picks the "best looking" answer, which is often wrong. The monkey has no idea what looks good and what doesn't, so will consistently be lucky about 20-25% of the time.
2. Test takers will eliminate answer choices from the guessing pool based on a hunch or intuition. Simple but correct answers often get excluded, leaving a 0% chance of being correct. The monkey has no clue, and often gets lucky with the best choice.

This is why the process of elimination endorsed by most test courses is flawed and detrimental to your performance- test takers don't guess, they make an ignorant stab in the dark that is usually worse than random.

$5 Challenge

Let me introduce one of the most valuable ideas of this course- the $5 challenge:

You only mark your "best guess" if you are willing to bet $5 on it.
You only eliminate choices from guessing if you are willing to bet $5 on it.

Why $5? Five dollars is an amount of money that is small yet not insignificant, and can really add up fast (20 questions could cost you $100). Likewise, each answer choice on one question of the test will have a small impact on your overall score, but it can really add up to a lot of points in the end.

The process of elimination IS valuable. The following shows your chance of guessing it right:

If you eliminate wrong answer choices until only this many answer choices remain:	1	2	3
Chance of getting it correct:	100%	50%	33%

However, if you accidentally eliminate the right answer or go on a hunch for an incorrect answer, your chances drop dramatically: to 0%. By guessing among all the answer choices, you are GUARANTEED to have a shot at the right answer.

That's why the $5 test is so valuable- if you give up the advantage and safety of a pure guess, it had better be worth the risk.

What we still haven't covered is how to be sure that whatever guess you make is truly random. Here's the easiest way:

Always pick the first answer choice among those remaining.

Such a technique means that you have decided, **before you see a single test question**, exactly how you are going to guess- and since the order of choices tells you nothing about which one is correct, this guessing technique is perfectly random.

This section is not meant to scare you away from making educated guesses or eliminating choices- you just need to define when a choice is worth eliminating. The $5 test, along with a pre-defined random guessing strategy, is the best way to make sure you reap all of the benefits of guessing.

Secret Key #3 – Practice Smarter, Not Harder

Many test takers delay the test preparation process because they dread the awful amounts of practice time they think necessary to succeed on the test. We have refined an effective method that will take you only a fraction of the time.

There are a number of "obstacles" in your way to succeed. Among these are answering questions, finishing in time, and mastering test-taking strategies. All must be executed on the day of the test at peak performance, or your score will suffer. The test is a mental marathon that has a large impact on your future.

Just like a marathon runner, it is important to work your way up to the full challenge. So first you just worry about questions, and then time, and finally strategy:

Success Strategy

1. Find a good source for practice tests.
2. If you are willing to make a larger time investment, consider using more than one study guide- often the different approaches of multiple authors will help you "get" difficult concepts.
3. Take a practice test with no time constraints, with all study helps "open book." Take your time with questions and focus on applying strategies.
4. Take a practice test with time constraints, with all guides "open book."
5. Take a final practice test with no open material and time limits

If you have time to take more practice tests, just repeat step 5. By gradually exposing yourself to the full rigors of the test environment, you will condition your mind to the stress of test day and maximize your success.

Secret Key #4 – Prepare, Don't Procrastinate

Let me state an obvious fact: if you take the test three times, you will get three different scores. This is due to the way you feel on test day, the level of preparedness you have, and, despite the test writers' claims to the contrary, some tests WILL be easier for you than others.

Since your future depends so much on your score, you should maximize your chances of success. In order to maximize the likelihood of success, you've got to prepare in advance. This means taking practice tests and spending time learning the information and test taking strategies you will need to succeed.

Never take the test as a "practice" test, expecting that you can just take it again if you need to. Feel free to take sample tests on your own, but when you go to take the official test, be prepared, be focused, and do your best the first time!

Secret Key #5 – Test Yourself

Everyone knows that time is money. There is no need to spend too much of your time or too little of your time preparing for the test. You should only spend as much of your precious time preparing as is necessary for you to get the score you need.

Once you have taken a practice test under real conditions of time constraints, then you will know if you are ready for the test or not.

If you have scored extremely high the first time that you take the practice test, then there is not much point in spending countless hours studying. You are already there.

Benchmark your abilities by retaking practice tests and seeing how much you have improved. Once you score high enough to guarantee success, then you are ready.

If you have scored well below where you need, then knuckle down and begin studying in earnest. Check your improvement regularly through the use of practice tests under real conditions. Above all, don't worry, panic, or give up. The key is perseverance!

Then, when you go to take the test, remain confident and remember how well you did on the practice tests. If you can score high enough on a practice test, then you can do the same on the real thing.

General Strategies

The most important thing you can do is to ignore your fears and jump into the test immediately- do not be overwhelmed by any strange-sounding terms. You have to jump into the test like jumping into a pool- all at once is the easiest way.

Make Predictions

As you read and understand the question, try to guess what the answer will be. Remember that several of the answer choices are wrong, and once you begin reading them, your mind will immediately become cluttered with answer choices designed to throw you off. Your mind is typically the most focused immediately after you have read the question and digested its contents. If you can, try to predict what the correct answer will be. You may be surprised at what you can predict.

Quickly scan the choices and see if your prediction is in the listed answer choices. If it is, then you can be quite confident that you have the right answer. It still won't hurt to check the other answer choices, but most of the time, you've got it!

Answer the Question

It may seem obvious to only pick answer choices that answer the question, but the test writers can create some excellent answer choices that are wrong. Don't pick an answer just because it sounds right, or you believe it to be true. It MUST answer the question. Once you've made your selection, always go back and check it against the question and make sure that you didn't misread the question, and the answer choice does answer the question posed.

Benchmark

After you read the first answer choice, decide if you think it sounds correct or not. If it doesn't, move on to the next answer choice. If it does, mentally mark that answer choice. This doesn't mean that you've definitely selected it as your answer choice; it just means that it's the best you've seen thus far. Go ahead and read the next choice. If the next choice is worse than the one you've already selected, keep going to the next answer choice. If the next choice is better than the choice you've already selected, mentally mark the new answer choice as your best guess.

The first answer choice that you select becomes your standard. Every other answer choice must be benchmarked against that standard. That choice is correct until proven otherwise by another answer choice beating it out. Once you've decided that no other answer choice seems as good, do one final check to ensure that your answer choice answers the question posed.

Valid Information

Don't discount any of the information provided in the question. Every piece of information may be necessary to determine the correct answer. None of the information in the question is there to throw you off (while the answer choices will certainly have information to throw you off). If two seemingly unrelated topics are discussed, don't ignore either. You can be confident there is a relationship, or it wouldn't be included in the question, and you are probably going to have to determine what that relationship is to find the answer.

Avoid "Fact Traps"

Don't get distracted by a choice that is factually true. Your search is for the answer that answers the question. Stay focused and don't fall for an answer that is true but incorrect. Always go back to the question and make sure you're choosing an answer that actually answers the question and is not just a true statement. An answer can be factually correct, but it MUST answer the question asked. Additionally, two answers can both be seemingly correct, so be sure to read all of the answer choices, and make sure that you get the one that BEST answers the question.

Milk the Question

Some of the questions may throw you completely off. They might deal with a subject you have not been exposed to, or one that you haven't reviewed in years. While your lack of knowledge about the subject will be a hindrance, the question itself can give you many clues that will help you find the correct answer. Read the question carefully and look for clues. Watch particularly for adjectives and nouns describing difficult terms or words that you don't recognize. Regardless of if you completely understand a word or not, replacing it with a synonym either provided or one you more familiar with may help you to understand what the questions are asking. Rather than wracking your mind about specific detailed information concerning a difficult term or word, try to use mental substitutes that are easier to understand.

The Trap of Familiarity

Don't just choose a word because you recognize it. On difficult questions, you may not recognize a number of words in the answer choices. The test writers don't put "make-believe" words on the test; so don't think that just because you only recognize all the words in one answer choice means that answer choice must be correct. If you only recognize words in one answer choice, then focus on that one. Is it correct? Try your best to determine if it is correct. If it is, that is great, but if it doesn't, eliminate it. Each word and answer choice you eliminate increases your chances of getting the question correct, even if you then have to guess among the unfamiliar choices.

Eliminate Answers

Eliminate choices as soon as you realize they are wrong. But be careful! Make sure you consider all of the possible answer choices. Just because one appears right, doesn't mean that the next one won't be even better! The test writers will usually put more than one good answer choice for every question, so read all of them. Don't worry if you are stuck between two that seem right. By getting down to just two remaining possible choices, your odds are now 50/50. Rather than wasting too much time, play the odds. You are guessing, but guessing wisely, because you've been able to knock out some of the answer choices that you know are wrong. If you are eliminating choices and realize that the last answer choice you are left with is also obviously wrong, don't panic. Start over and consider each choice again. There may easily be something that you missed the first time and will realize on the second pass.

Tough Questions

If you are stumped on a problem or it appears too hard or too difficult, don't waste time. Move on! Remember though, if you can quickly check for obviously incorrect answer choices, your chances of guessing correctly are greatly improved. Before you completely give up, at least try to knock out a couple of possible answers. Eliminate what you can and then guess at the remaining answer choices before moving on.

Brainstorm

If you get stuck on a difficult question, spend a few seconds quickly brainstorming. Run through the complete list of possible answer choices. Look at each choice and ask yourself, "Could this answer the question satisfactorily?" Go through each answer choice and consider it independently of the other. By systematically going through all possibilities, you may find something that you would otherwise overlook. Remember that when you get stuck, it's important to try to keep moving.

Read Carefully

Understand the problem. Read the question and answer choices carefully. Don't miss the question because you misread the terms. You have plenty of time to read each question thoroughly and make sure you understand what is being asked. Yet a happy medium must be attained, so don't waste too much time. You must read carefully, but efficiently.

Face Value

When in doubt, use common sense. Always accept the situation in the problem at face value. Don't read too much into it. These problems will not require you to make huge leaps of logic. The test writers aren't trying to throw you off with a cheap trick. If you have to go beyond creativity and make a leap of logic in order to have an answer choice answer the question, then you should look at the other answer choices. Don't overcomplicate the problem by creating theoretical relationships or explanations that will warp time or space. These are normal problems rooted in reality. It's just that the applicable relationship or explanation may not be readily apparent and you have to figure things out. Use your common sense to interpret anything that isn't clear.

Prefixes

If you're having trouble with a word in the question or answer choices, try dissecting it. Take advantage of every clue that the word might include. Prefixes and suffixes can be a huge help. Usually they allow you to determine a basic meaning. Pre- means before, post- means after, pro - is positive, de- is negative. From these prefixes and suffixes, you can get an idea of the general meaning of the word and try to put it into context. Beware though of any traps. Just because con is the opposite of pro, doesn't necessarily mean congress is the opposite of progress!

Hedge Phrases

Watch out for critical "hedge" phrases, such as likely, may, can, will often, sometimes, often, almost, mostly, usually, generally, rarely, sometimes. Question writers insert these hedge phrases to cover every possibility. Often an answer choice will be wrong simply because it leaves no room for exception. Avoid answer choices that have definitive words like "exactly," and "always".

Switchback Words

Stay alert for "switchbacks". These are the words and phrases frequently used to alert you to shifts in thought. The most common switchback word is "but". Others include although, however, nevertheless, on the other hand, even though, while, in spite of, despite, regardless of.

New Information

Correct answer choices will rarely have completely new information included. Answer choices typically are straightforward reflections of the material asked about and will directly relate to the question. If a new piece of information is included in an answer choice that doesn't even seem to relate to the topic being asked about, then that answer choice is likely incorrect. All of the information needed to answer the question is usually provided for you, and so you should not have to make guesses that are unsupported or choose answer choices that require unknown information that cannot be reasoned on its own.

Time Management

On technical questions, don't get lost on the technical terms. Don't spend too much time on any one question. If you don't know what a term means, then since you don't have a dictionary, odds are you aren't going to get much further. You should immediately recognize terms as whether or not you know them. If you don't, work with the other clues that you have, the other answer choices and terms provided, but don't waste too much time trying to figure out a difficult term.

Contextual Clues

Look for contextual clues. An answer can be right but not correct. The contextual clues will help you find the answer that is most right and is correct. Understand the context in which a phrase or statement is made. This will help you make important distinctions.

Don't Panic

Panicking will not answer any questions for you. Therefore, it isn't helpful. When you first see the question, if your mind goes blank, take a deep breath. Force yourself to mechanically go through the steps of solving the problem and using the strategies you've learned.

Pace Yourself

Don't get clock fever. It's easy to be overwhelmed when you're looking at a page full of questions, your mind is full of random thoughts and feeling confused, and the clock is ticking down faster than you would like. Calm down and maintain the pace that you have set for yourself. As long as you are on track by monitoring your pace, you are guaranteed to have enough time for yourself. When you get to the last few minutes of the test, it may seem like you won't have enough time left, but if you only have as many questions as you should have left at that point, then you're right on track!

Answer Selection

The best way to pick an answer choice is to eliminate all of those that are wrong, until only one is left and confirm that is the correct answer. Sometimes though, an answer choice may immediately look right. Be careful! Take a second to make sure that the other choices are not equally obvious.

Don't make a hasty mistake. There are only two times that you should stop before checking other answers. First is when you are positive that the answer choice you have selected is correct. Second is when time is almost out and you have to make a quick guess!

Check Your Work

Since you will probably not know every term listed and the answer to every question, it is important that you get credit for the ones that you do know. Don't miss any questions through careless mistakes. If at all possible, try to take a second to look back over your answer selection and make sure you've selected the correct answer choice and haven't made a costly careless mistake (such as marking an answer choice that you didn't mean to mark). This quick double check should more than pay for itself in caught mistakes for the time it costs.

Beware of Directly Quoted Answers

Sometimes an answer choice will repeat word for word a portion of the question or reference section. However, beware of such exact duplication – it may be a trap! More than likely, the correct choice will paraphrase or summarize a point, rather than being exactly the same wording.

Slang

Scientific sounding answers are better than slang ones. An answer choice that begins "To compare the outcomes..." is much more likely to be correct than one that begins "Because some people insisted..."

Extreme Statements

Avoid wild answers that throw out highly controversial ideas that are proclaimed as established fact. An answer choice that states the "process should be used in certain situations, if..." is much more likely to be correct than one that states the "process should be discontinued completely." The first is a calm rational statement and doesn't even make a definitive, uncompromising stance, using a hedge word "if" to provide wiggle room, whereas the second choice is a radical idea and far more extreme.

Answer Choice Families

When you have two or more answer choices that are direct opposites or parallels, one of them is usually the correct answer. For instance, if one answer choice states "x increases" and another answer choice states "x decreases" or "y increases," then those two or three answer choices are very similar in construction and fall into the same family of answer choices. A family of answer choices is when two or three answer choices are very similar in construction, and yet often have a directly opposite meaning. Usually the correct answer choice will be in that family of answer choices. The "odd man out" or answer choice that doesn't seem to fit the parallel construction of the other answer choices is more likely to be incorrect.

Special Report: Additional Bonus Material

Due to our efforts to try to keep this book to a manageable length, we've created a link that will give you access to all of your additional bonus material.

Please visit http://www.mometrix.com/bonus948/lare to access the information.

CPSIA information can be obtained
at www.ICGtesting.com
Printed in the USA
BVHW011053120819
555663BV00020B/1771/P